The Screwtape Letters and the Catechism

THE SCREWTAPE LETTERS AND THE *CATECHISM*

Recognizing Temptation, Battling Sin, and Growing in Spiritual Courage

Marlon De La Torre, PhD

Our Sunday Visitor
Huntington, Indiana

Nihil Obstat
Msgr. Michael Heintz, Ph.D.
Censor Librorum

Imprimatur
✠ Kevin C. Rhoades
Bishop of Fort Wayne-South Bend
December 13, 2023

The *Nihil Obstat* and *Imprimatur* are official declarations that a book is free from doctrinal or moral error. It is not implied that those who have granted the *Nihil Obstat* and *Imprimatur* agree with the contents, opinions, or statements expressed.

29 28 27 26 25 2 3 4 5 6 7 8 9

Our Sunday Visitor Publishing Division
Our Sunday Visitor, Inc.
200 Noll Plaza
Huntington, IN 46750
www.osv.com
1-800-348-2440

ISBN: 978-1-68192-547-9 (Inventory No. T2779)
1. RELIGION—Christian Theology—General.
2. RELIGION—Christianity—Catechisms.
3. RELIGION—Christianity—Catholic.

eISBN: 978-1-68192-548-6
LCCN: 2024931707

Cover and interior design: Amanda Falk
Cover credit: AdobeStock

PRINTED IN THE UNITED STATES OF AMERICA

To my wife, and to our children: Miguel, Gabriela, Maria, and Gianna, the greatest gift a father could have.

Contents

Introduction

There is a seductive voice that lurks among us, and as a result of the sin of our first parents, we are all susceptible to its lies. When Adam and Eve heard the first whispers of that cunning voice, they chose to turn toward it — away from God. The original sin opened the door to the Devil, and as a result, we now encounter a daily battle between good and evil in our world and our souls.

This spiritual battle is ongoing because the Devil will never cease trying to destroy any relationship you and I may have with Jesus Christ. Even though the Devil and his fallen angels were created to be good, they made a choice to reject God and thus banished themselves from the kingdom of heaven.

The free choice of the Devil and his fallen legion of demons is the same choice — the same temptation — we face every day. The Devil and his angels will try to entice us to choose them above Jesus Christ.

At the heart of the Fall of our first parents is the complete rejection of God. The Devil's false promise was that Adam and Eve would be like God if they ate the fruit of the tree of the garden that God had forbidden them to eat. Instead, they lost the intimacy of their original relationship with him.

St. John Vianney describes the prevalence of temptation as follows:

> It is most unfortunate for ourselves if we do not know

> that we are tempted in almost all our actions, at one time by pride, by vanity, by the good opinion which we think people should have of us, at another by jealousy, by hatred, and by revenge. At other times the Devil comes to us with the foulest and most impure images. You see that even in our prayers he distracts us and turns our minds this way and that.

St. John the Evangelist reminds us that "the reason the Son of God appeared was to destroy the works of the devil" (1 Jn 3:8; *Catechism of the Catholic Church,* 394). Jesus identifies the Devil as "a murderer from the beginning" (Jn 8:44), and we encounter in Sacred Scripture just how far the Devil is willing to go to convince Jesus Christ not to complete his Father's mission on earth (see Mt 4:1–11). If the Devil sought to tempt Jesus, then anyone who claims to be a follower of Jesus Christ should expect the same spiritual attack. The Devil has no authority over us since he is not the author of creation, nor is he capable of controlling us. But he can distract us and cause us to wound ourselves spiritually, thus distancing us from Jesus Christ and from our Father's unending love.

Padre Pio describes the Devil as a rabid dog tied to a chain; beyond the length of the chain, he cannot seize anyone. But we must keep at a distance, for if we approach too near, we let ourselves be caught. Remember that the Devil has only one door by which to enter the soul: the will.

Why does God allow the Devil to roam the earth seeking the destruction of souls? God in his infinite goodness allows the Devil to roam the cosmos because his greater plan of salvation awaits us, no matter what misery the Devil may cause spiritually or physically. God allows this as part of his divine providence that guides us to our ultimate end, which is eternal life with our Father in heaven.

Part of our journey to heaven is the embrace of our redemptive suffering, more commonly referred to as "carrying our cross." The Devil roams the world because God permits it, not because the Devil has authority over God. The Devil was created by God as a pure, holy angel, but he chose to rebel by preferring himself over God. The Devil's act of disobedience when he sought to be like God is what separated him from God.

God did not destroy the Devil but instead banished him from receiving the eternal gift of grace. Now the Devil roams the earth seeking the destruction of the souls God created. After the introduction of original sin, Adam and Eve became subject to the pain of sin and death, which the Devil is happy to provide.

But God offered Adam and Eve and all their descendants the opportunity to regain their identity as his children. God's salvific plan includes man's battle with sin, which results in spiritual and physical suffering. If properly ordered toward God, this suffering prepares us to be judged and hopefully received by God in heaven.

C. S. Lewis's *The Screwtape Letters* is a literary masterpiece that helps us understand the battle between good and evil. Lewis grew up in Belfast, Northern Ireland, with a quiet antagonism toward Christianity. His genuine friendship with the great J. R. R. Tolkien and Tolkien's witness of faith finally brought Lewis to embrace Christianity. His newfound faith led him to investigate the battle between good and evil. He knew all too well how easily man's faith can be swayed away from God by the Devil.

It is important to understand that C. S. Lewis was not Catholic, and his Anglican faith did not include the same sacramental awareness or understanding of our relationship with God that the Catholic Church teaches. Also, his religious instruction was not associated with a particular Christian catechism. Though Lewis did not write *The Screwtape Letters* to be read in conjunction with the *Catechism of the Catholic Church*, the application of the *Catechism* to his work fills in many doctrinal gaps that Lewis would not have been able to address.

The Screwtape Letters leads us into the perspective of the Devil through a dialogue between a senior demon, Screwtape, and his underling, Wormwood, who is tasked to lead "the patient" — an ordinary man who represents you and me — away from "the Enemy," meaning God. We tend to forget that the Devil is a pure spirit, which means that he is not limited by time or space. How are you and I supposed to battle a pure spirit whose only purpose is to keep us from developing an active relationship with Jesus Christ? This is the question at the heart of *The Screwtape Letters.*

The premise behind my book is to provide hope for anyone who has been tempted by the Devil or struggled with the daily battle against sin — that is, all of us. But we don't just want to see how the Devil works to lead us away from God; we also want to know how we can respond to temptations in faith. The *Catechism of the Catholic Church* provides us with this answer. The *Catechism* reveals God's love for us through its faithful expression of Christian doctrine, the whole purpose of which is to strengthen our relationship with Jesus Christ. It serves as an instrument of grace to help us combat the works of the Devil. The Deposit of Faith revealed in the *Catechism* is perfectly suited to address the deposit of sin.

The *Catechism* is a direct reflection and gift of the Word of God revealed through Jesus Christ to convey God's love to all humanity. When we juxtapose *The Screwtape Letters* with the *Catechism*, we encounter a battle between the Word of God and the Devil himself.

Reading *The Screwtape Letters* in conjunction with the *Catechism of the Catholic Church* provides a helpful understanding of how the Devil tempts us to sin so that we can escape his clutches and live the grace-filled lives God has planned for us. The dialogue between Wormwood and Screwtape will help us develop keen insight to avoid the near occasion of sin and prepare us for our daily spiritual battle.

The Screwtape Letters is as relevant today as it was when it was first published in 1942 because it addresses the age-old battle of virtue and grace against vice and sin. More than sixty years after Lewis's death, we see that *The Screwtape Letters* has withstood the test of time. It continues to provide us with a prudent understanding of the battle between good and evil and how our own lives revolve around this spiritual drama of faith.

I hope that this book will serve as a catechetical resource to strengthen your relationship with Jesus Christ and help you avoid the near occasion of sin, as well as serve as a spiritual devotional. Above all, remember that Jesus is always inviting us to receive His "love that never ends" (CCC 25).

Chapter 1
Faith and Relativism

Now faith is the assurance of things hoped for, the conviction of things not seen. For by it the men of old received divine approval. By faith we understand that the world was created by the word of God, so that what is seen was made out of things which do not appear.

— *Hebrews 11:1–3*

> *Your man ... doesn't think of doctrines as primarily "true" or "false," but as "academic" or "practical," "outworn" or "contemporary," "conventional" or "ruthless." Jargon, not argument is your best ally in keeping him from the Church. ... Even if a particular train of thought can be twisted so as to end in our favor, you will find that you have been strengthening in your patient the fatal habit of attending to universal issues and withdrawing his attention from the stream of immediate sense experiences. Your business is to fix his attention on the stream.*
>
> The Screwtape Letters, 1

In his first letter, Screwtape tells Wormwood that the patient (the person he is assigned to tempt) views Christian doctrines as outworn and impractical. He encourages Wormwood to keep the patient away from the Church through meaningless words and to distract him from reality by causing him to focus only on what he can see and feel. If the Devil can convince us to view Christian doctrine as just one other teaching or way of thinking among many equal belief systems, then he can erode our faith because it is no longer rooted in God's Truth.

DEBUNKING SCREWTAPE

Screwtape urges Wormwood to teach the patient the art of distraction. The Devil would like nothing else than to distract us and ultimately separate us from our relationship with God. All of us can relate to the "patient" in some way when we try to focus our attention on God, only to be distracted. The nature of any distraction can be associated with our inclination to sin. Our distractions can become more important than our relationship with God, and the Devil tempts us in this way especially when we attempt to build a relationship with God through prayer.

Keep in mind that the Devil is very subtle in distracting us from forming an active relationship with God. He will use many things in our lives to distract us — concern for a family member or a project at work all of a sudden saturates our mind and requires more attention than our time with God. The devil starts out subtly, distracting us with good things, but over time, he would like nothing more than to tempt us to place more attention on our own personal needs than those of others. The growth of the god of social media, for instance, and the need to be recognized for silly stunts has become for many people more important than an intimate, loving relationship with God.

Prayer (whether the recitation of a Rosary, divine mercy chaplet, quiet time in adoration, or asking for the intercession of the Holy Spirit in our daily lives) can help us overcome these temptations. Quiet, contemplative prayer, where we focus on the passion of Jesus Christ, may serve as an antidote to the noises that inundate our lives through music, video images, and personalized media sites. Prayer helps us avoid distraction and place our focus on the Holy Spirit as the messenger and voice of God.

What begin as small distractions from prayer can grow into a habit of distraction from reality. Ultimately, the Devil wants to convince us that there is no difference between a world with God and one without him. If he can do this, then he can lead us to wonder why we should practice any form of faith at all. In *The Screwtape Letters*, Screwtape is so threatened by the possibility of the patient's faith in "the Enemy" that he urges Wormwood to avoid all potential avenues for the patient to argue about faith, reason, or the Christian worldview, even if he takes the opposing side, because the argument itself will cause the patient to ponder moral questions. The battle that we encounter in this first letter provides a glimpse of how far the Devil is willing to go to distract us from having a relationship with God.

How do we begin to debunk Screwtape?

First, we must remember that all of us were created in the image and likeness of God and not in the image of the Devil. Because we bear God's image, it is part of our human nature to seek and worship the Divine. More specifically, we are called to worship the one, true God. The *Catechism of the Catholic Church* reminds us that you and I can know and understand God as the Creator by natural reason (see 50). This is important because it is exactly what the Devil does not want us to do. He wants to keep us from wrestling with big questions or arguing to find the truth. The more we distance ourselves from the love of God and our natural inclination to ponder the world he created, the more easily we fall into the Devil's snares.

The *Catechism* provides us with spiritual ammunition by

reminding us that the obedience of faith means to hear and submit freely to the Word of God (144). We can trust that God will never stop speaking to us even if we fall into sin. God is not bound by sin, so he can work even through our sinful behaviors by reminding us that he will always love us. This strengthens our resolve to believe in him, knowing that he is always there.

Faith and obedience are gifts that allow us to listen to God more intently and thus utilize our ability to reason to arrive at the truth of God as our eternal Father in heaven.

APPLICATION OF THE *CATECHISM*

Instead of employing an argument, which can sharpen both mind and faith, Screwtape instructs Wormwood to lead the patient into relativism. Relativism is the view that all truth is subjective, and that as a result there are no moral absolutes. For the relativist, faith is unnecessary because one's personal feelings and opinions are all that matter. The premise behind relativism is that whatever an individual thinks or feels is right. According to relativism, there is no need to believe in a universal truth or adhere to a certain way of living. Hence, moral or ethical norms do not apply in our life, and faith itself is unnecessary and inconsequential.

The Devil seeks to guide us to have faith that centers on ourselves rather than on God. Faith, on the other hand, is our adherence to God and his truth (CCC 150). It is a desire for the Divine that leads us to ponder the questions surrounding our existence. God uses that longing to reveal himself in love to us, his children, and invite us to know him. Faith is our response to God's love by which we commit our lives to him. When we freely choose to assent to God, we also assent to his truth. The key to debunking Screwtape's relativism is to pose the reasonable proposition that God is both knowable and absolute.

A prudent way to avoid the spiritual trap of relativism is to renounce any negative spiritual habit or behavior such as pride, envy, jealousy, or unholy anger in the name of Jesus Christ. Such habits may lead us to see the truth as merely a matter of opinion, or to overlook the gravity of sin as an offensive act of our will against God.

Simply say: "In the name of Jesus, I renounce [whatever sin may be damaging my relationship with Christ]." The *Catechism* again serves us well in combating the Devil, as it reveals that everyone — including you and me — "is called to enter the kingdom" (543). Let us not forget that "Jesus invites *sinners* to the table of the kingdom" (545). God has inscribed a law into our heart to help us have a properly formed conscience. This law of conscience helps us to do good and avoid evil (1776).

DISCUSSION QUESTIONS

- In what ways can I combat distractions and develop my desire for God?
- How can meditation on the life and death of Jesus Christ help me avoid being spiritually distracted?
- How can this meditation help me combat the temptations of relativism?

The *Anima Christi* (meaning "Soul of Christ") is a prayer attributed to St. Ignatius of Loyola that asks for Jesus' help, guidance, strength, and protection:

> Soul of Christ, sanctify me.
> Body of Christ, save me.
> Blood of Christ, inebriate me.
> Water from the side of Christ, wash me.
> Passion of Christ, strengthen me.
> O good Jesus, hear me.
> Within your wounds, conceal me.

Do not permit me to be parted from you.
From the evil foe protect me.
At the hour of my death call me.
And bid me come to you,
To praise you with all your saints
Forever and ever.
Amen.

How might praying the *Anima Christi* help me remain spiritually focused as a disciple of Jesus Christ?

• • • • •

MEDITATION

(From *A Treatise on Christian Perfection* by St. Gregory of Nyssa)*

The life of the Christian has three distinguishing aspects: deeds, words, and thought. Thought comes first, then words, since our words express openly the interior conclusions of the mind. Finally, after thoughts and words, comes action, for our deeds carry out what the mind has conceived. So when one of these results in our acting or speaking or thinking, we must make sure that all our thoughts, words, and deeds are controlled by the divine ideal, the revelation of Christ. For then our thoughts, words, and deeds will not fall short of the nobility of their implications.

What then must we do, we who have been found worthy of the name of Christ? Each of us must examine his thoughts, words and deeds, to see whether they are directed toward Christ or are turned away from him.

*PG 46, 283–286, quoted in *Liturgy of the Hours*, Tuesday of the Twelfth Week in Ordinary Time, Office of Readings, Second Reading.

This examination is carried out in various ways. Our deeds or our thoughts or our words are not in harmony with Christ if they issue from passion. They then bear the mark of the enemy who smears the pearl of the heart with the slime of passion, dimming and even destroying the luster of the precious stone.

On the other hand, if they are free from and untainted by every passionate inclination, they are directed toward Christ, the author and source of peace. He is like a pure, untainted stream. If you draw from him the thoughts in your mind and the inclinations of your heart, you will show a likeness to Christ, your source and origin, as the gleaming water in a jar resembles the flowing water from which it was obtained.

For the purity of Christ and the purity that is manifest in our hearts are identical. Christ's purity, however, is the fountainhead; ours has its source in him and flows out of him. Our life is stamped with the beauty of his thought. The inner and the outer man are harmonized in a kind of music. The mind of Christ is the controlling influence that inspires us to moderation and goodness in our behavior. As I see it, Christian perfection consists in this: sharing the titles which express the meaning of Christ's name, we bring out this meaning in our minds, our prayers and our way of life.

Chapter 2
Bearing False Witness and Authentic Conversion

But as for you, man of God, shun all this; aim at righteousness, godliness, faith, love, steadfastness, gentleness. Fight the good fight of the faith; take hold of the eternal life to which you were called when you made the good confession in the presence of many witnesses.

— *1 Timothy 6:11–12*

> *I note with grave displeasure that your patient has become a Christian. ... There is no need to despair; hundreds of these adult converts have been reclaimed after a brief sojourn in the Enemy's camp and are now with us. All the* habits *of the patient, both mental and bodily, are still in our favor. ... Work hard, then, on the disappointment or anticlimax which is certainly coming to the patient during his first weeks as a churchman. The Enemy allows this disappointment to occur on the threshold of every human endeavor.*
>
> The Screwtape Letters, 2

In his second letter, Screwtape is very disappointed that Wormwood's "patient" has become a Christian. He reminds Wormwood about impending consequences due to his failure to keep the patient from becoming Christian. However, Screwtape does not seem too bothered by this new development because he expects the patient to fall back into his old, sinful ways. Screwtape is betting that the patient will ultimately fall prey to his sinful habits and desires rather than continue to worship God. In other words, it's only a matter of time before the patient will sin again.

DEBUNKING SCREWTAPE

When we begin to develop a relationship with Jesus Christ, the journey will involve peaks and valleys, joys and sorrows. Joys when we sense his Presence, especially in the Holy Eucharist, and dismay when it appears that he is not there. A relationship with Jesus requires trust, openness, faith, and work because we are constantly tempted to turn away from him. Every day, the distractions of the world pull us to love our own pleasure more than God.

According to Screwtape, there is no hope in becoming Christian because all of us will eventually fall back into sinful habits, thus negating our Christian faith. The Devil encourages us to be Christian hypocrites and bear false witness to our very selves. But the Devil refuses to understand that God is both all-merciful and all-loving. God never puts on a false face and never bears false witness. His love is reflected in the gift of our free will, by which we can choose right over wrong. Our free will is anchored by the gift of God's grace that helps us to choose virtue over vice. Even if we fall back toward a sinful inclination, it does not mean that our faith is destroyed. We possess the ability — through our own free will — to start over. God, who created us in his own image and likeness, does not leave us alone, and he reveals his love for us through his Son Jesus Christ.

Conversion of our lives to God the Father, God the Son, and

God the Holy Spirit requires an act of faith, which, as the *Catechism* reminds us, is a human act (154). The Holy Spirit serves as a nourishing guide who strengthens our faith in God. Faith, if honestly sought, demands to see the truth, even when the truth may not be visible. Within the context of the Mass, for example, we encounter the living God through his Son Jesus Christ, where our faith intersects with the love of Christ revealed in the Holy Eucharist. The mystery of Jesus' sacrifice on the cross becomes a visible reality when we participate in the reception of His Body and Blood.

APPLICATION OF THE *CATECHISM*

The *Catechism* teaches that we all go through a progression of faith. First, it is a gift from God himself. He provides us with the gift of faith, especially through His Word because study of Sacred Scripture is an important way to strengthen our faith (162). Faith invites us toward conversion, which is an important first step on our journey to heaven. The gift of faith provides us with the opportunity to develop a relationship with God, allowing us to recognize that we need to be healed by him in order for our faith to grow.

The *Catechism* reminds us that we should not bear false witness against our neighbor (2464). The eighth commandment directs us not to misrepresent the truth about others or ourselves. Respecting our human dignity enables us to respect those around us and ourselves, and it allows us to seek a deeper conversion to Jesus Christ and his Church. When we experience a sincere conversion of faith to Jesus Christ, our human senses mature in their ability to seek good and avoid evil.

DISCUSSION QUESTIONS

› How does my lack of faith distract me from loving my neighbor as a child of God?

› How can I begin to turn away from sin and dedicate my life to God?

• • • • •

MEDITATION
(St. Charbel Makhlouf)

You will understand the depth of the mystery of existence through the light of the eternal Spirit that is in you. Do not seek to comprehend the truth through your senses, for then you will be limited by the limits of these senses.

Know that your senses exist so that you may love through them, and not so that you may love them. … Transcend your senses and do not drown in them; reach through them to the truth as the ray of light reaches through crystal. …

True joy is not the joy of the senses, true joy transcends your senses, and goes past them to the heart of the light where you would drown in the heart of God, see His light and melt in His love. Go beyond your senses and go past them, go beyond yourself, and then you will touch the edge of the light. Whenever you want to look to the outside, close your eyes and look to the inside, then start seeing the outside more clearly. Whenever you want to hear, cover your ears and listen to the inner voice; then you will start hearing better. Guide your senses to glorify God, and do not let your senses lead you to glorify His creatures. Love to the point of self-sacrifice: blood is the only ink with which love is written, and everything else is only ink on paper. In Christ, every man is a word in the mouth of God so that all humanity becomes a song of love.

Chapter 3

Honor Yourself or Honor God?

Do you not know that you are God's temple and that God's Spirit dwells in you? If any one destroys God's temple, God will destroy him. For God's temple is holy, and that temple you are.

— 1 Corinthians 3:16–17

> *It is, no doubt, impossible to prevent his praying for his mother, but we have means of rendering the prayers innocuous. Make sure they are always very "spiritual," that he is always concerned with the state of her soul and never with her rheumatism. … His attention will be kept on what he regards as her sins by which … he can be induced to mean any of her actions that are inconvenient or irritating to himself.*
>
> The Screwtape Letters, 3

In his third letter, Screwtape encourages Wormwood to foster a destructive relationship between the patient and his mother.

What Wormwood dreads most is that the patient and his mother will develop a loving relationship based on "the Enemy" — Jesus Christ.

Screwtape is also determined to develop a disordered sense of prayer within the patient. Specifically, Screwtape wants to render meaningless any attempt by the patient to pray for his mother. He wants the patient to focus on his mother's sins rather than her identity as a child of God. If Wormwood can achieve this, he can convince the patient that his negative and uncharitable behavior toward his mother is justified, as he will earnestly believe that her behavior is far worse than his own.

DEBUNKING SCREWTAPE

We are created out of love. Because we carry the image and likeness of God, we are called to use our free will to act in accordance with the Father's love and shun any behavior that may contradict or reject God's love for us. Since every single person on earth bears the image and likeness of God, we have been endowed with a moral responsibility to respect the dignity of each human person.

The Devil is relentless in his quest to cause irreparable harm in our relationships with one another, especially with those closest to us. Parents are natural intercessors for their children, with whom they possess an intimate spiritual and physical bond. Mothers in particular both nurture and nourish their children in a way that protects and strengthens them. The role of a parent is to reflect and witness to God's love for his children.

Screwtape wants to fracture the loving, nurturing relationship between the patient and his mother because it reflects God's loving relationship as Abba, Father, to us, his children. When a parent-child relationship is wounded or fractured, it creates spiritual dissension, disunity, and lack of trust, all of which provide fertile ground for temptations and sin to grow. This is true of any relationship we may have with other people, from those closest to us (like parents and spouses) to those we know only slightly. Regardless of the nature of the relationship, when we demean a fellow human being, we deny his or her dignity as someone created in the image and likeness of God. Upholding that dignity "is an essential part of the proclamation of the kingdom" of God to which all the baptized are called (CCC 1427).

APPLICATION OF THE *CATECHISM*

Screwtape and Wormwood both fear God's hold on the patient in his desire to pray for his mother. When he prays, the patient is following the rule of faith — the structure and method of how every one of us believes in God as revealed in Sacred Tradition and Sacred Scripture through the Ten Commandments, in this case especially the fourth commandment to honor father and mother (2197–2200). The fourth commandment emphasizes the necessity for acts of charity toward our parents, who have been entrusted with the moral, doctrinal, and spiritual responsibility of raising their children on behalf of God.

The active practice of the rule of faith allows us to engage in a life of conversion toward Jesus Christ and openly proclaim the kingdom of God. When we choose to honor God and follow the rule of faith expressed in the Ten Commandments, it leads us away from evil to a radical conversion toward Jesus Christ and his Church. The words of Jesus in the Beatitudes call us to embrace the vision of God: "Blessed are the pure in heart, for they shall see God" (Mt 5:8).

DISCUSSION QUESTIONS

› How do I honor my parents, especially if they struggled to express their love for me?

› For what sins do I need to forgive my parents? For which of my own sins do I need to ask their forgiveness?

• • • • •

MEDITATION

(Prayer of St. John Damascene)

> O my God and my Lord Jesus Christ, lead me in your way that I may walk in your truth; gladden my heart that I may fear your holy name. O Lord so mighty in mercy, so gracious in your might, assist and comfort me; save me, for I put my trust in your holy name. In your wrath, do not let me perish, O Lord and Lover of Mankind, but show me your great mercy and compassion. O Physician and Healer of my soul, O merciful Savior, blot out all my transgressions, for in the depth of my heart I am sorry for having offended you. Grant me your grace, that I may avoid my earlier and evil ways; give me the strength, O Mighty One, to withstand the temptations before which I am weak; keep me under your protection, and under the shadow of your wings, so that I may serve you faithfully, praise you, and glorify your name all the days of my life. The Father is my hope, the Son my refuge, the Holy Spirit my shelter. O Holy Trinity, all glory to you! All my hope I place in you, O Mother of God; keep me under your protection. Amen.

Chapter 4
Authentic Prayer

He was praying in a certain place, and when he ceased, one of his disciples said to him, "Lord, teach us to pray."

— Luke 11:1

> *Keep the patient from the serious intention of praying altogether. ... This is best done by encouraging him to remember ... the parrot-like nature of his prayers in childhood. In reaction against that, he may be persuaded to aim at something entirely spontaneous ... and what this will actually mean to a beginner will be an effort to produce in himself a vaguely devotional* mood. ... *Whenever they are attending to the Enemy Himself, we are defeated, but there are ways of preventing them from doing so. The simplest is to turn their gaze away from Him towards themselves.*
>
> The Screwtape Letters, 4

In his fourth letter, Screwtape takes considerable time to discuss the painful subject of prayer with Wormwood. Screwtape wants Wormwood to keep the patient from developing an authentic prayer life. Even more, he strongly encourages Wormwood to keep the patient from praying altogether. He wants to cause the patient to regress in prayer by employing the art of distraction. This coincides with the earlier tactic that sought to have him ignore the presence of God altogether. Distraction will keep things that will lead the patient to pray to God out of his mind. Better still, if Wormwood can convince the patient to pray to something other than God, the mission will be accomplished.

DEBUNKING SCREWTAPE

It is important to understand that the Devil does not want us to pray to God, and he will stop at nothing to sway us away from speaking, praying, or walking with him. The reason is quite simple: The more we pray to God, the stronger our relationship with our Father in heaven grows. We become more aware of God's presence in our lives and affirm our identity as God's children created in his image and likeness. Every time we pray to Our Lord, we strengthen our ability to be in communion with him, which allows us to be receptive to his love. The virtue of love is the last thing that the Devil wants us to experience because it brings us closer to God and farther away from his temptations.

APPLICATION OF THE *CATECHISM*

The *Catechism* defines prayer as the "raising of one's mind and heart to God" (2559). St. Thérèse of Lisieux reminds us that "prayer is a surge of the heart; it is a simple look turned toward heaven, it is a cry of recognition and of love, embracing both trial and joy" (see 2558).

The Devil despises when a human being prays because it leads the person toward a more intimate relationship with God. Satan desires to cause confusion, complacency, and indifference in our relationship with God. The last thing the Devil wants is to see someone develop a relationship with Jesus Christ, the Son of God, through a faithful act of prayer.

True prayer comes from the heart (2562). In the heart, we encounter the source of why and how we pray, whether through meditation, contemplation, or adoration. The *Catechism* reminds us that the heart is the place of truth, where we choose life or death. It "is the place of encounter, because as image of God we live in relation, and it is the place of covenant" (2563).

Prayer is a genuine conversation with God and open communication with God's grace. The parable of the persistent friend in Luke 11:5–13 invites us to urgent prayer:

> And he said to them, "Which of you who has a friend will go to him at midnight and say to him, 'Friend, lend me three loaves; for a friend of mine has arrived on a journey, and I have nothing to set before him'; and he will answer from within, 'Do not bother me; the door is now shut, and my children are with me in bed; I cannot get up and give you anything'? I tell you, though he will not get up and give him anything because he is his friend, yet because of his importunity he will rise and give him whatever he needs. And I tell you, Ask, and it will be given you; seek, and you will find; knock, and it will be opened to you. For every one who asks receives, and he who seeks finds, and to him who knocks it will be opened. What father among you, if his son asks for a fish, will instead of a fish give him a serpent; or if he asks for an egg, will give him a scorpion? If you then, who are evil, know how to give good gifts to your children, how much more will the heavenly Father give the Holy Spirit to those who ask him!"

When we ask, seek, and finally knock, this persistence helps us grow in the habit of prayer. When we ask God to communicate with us, we seek to come into an intimate relationship with him.

Other parables in Scripture reinforce this theme of the urgency of prayer. The story of the widow in Luke 18:1–8 also shows it is necessary to pray always without ceasing and with the patience of faith. The parable of the Pharisee and the tax collector in Luke 18:9–14 demonstrates the necessity for humility in the heart that prays: "God, be merciful to me a sinner."

DISCUSSION QUESTIONS

- Why is trust important when we are praying to God?
- How is my heart a place of prayer, and what can I do to cultivate my heart as a place of encounter with God in prayer?

• • • • •

MEDITATION

The best prayer is the Our Father, also called the Lord's Prayer, which Jesus taught to his disciples. This prayer "is truly the summary of the whole gospel" (CCC 2761). St. Thomas Aquinas reminds us, "The Lord's Prayer is the most perfect of prayers" (2763).

> Our Father who art in heaven, hallowed be thy name; thy kingdom come, thy will be done on earth as it is in heaven. Give us this day our daily bread, and forgive us our trespasses, as we forgive those who trespass against us; and lead us not into temptation, but deliver us from evil. Amen.

Chapter 5
Despair and Hope

For in this hope we were saved. Now hope that is seen is not hope. For who hopes for what he sees? But if we hope for what we do not see, we wait for it with patience.

— *Romans 8:24–25*

> *For the first time in your career, you have tasted that wine which is the reward of all our labors — the anguish and bewilderment of a human soul — and it has gone to your head. ... Do not allow any temporary excitement to distract you from the real business of undermining faith and preventing the formation of virtues. ... In the meantime, I must warn you not to hope too much from a war.*
>
> The Screwtape Letters, 5

In his fifth letter, Screwtape warns Wormwood not to celebrate victory even though he has succeeded in distracting and distancing the patient from God. Any premature celebration may lead to the loss of the prey. Screwtape urges Wormwood to be calm, cool, and shrewd to secure the soul of the patient because this is the ultimate end. And this is where our battle with the Devil becomes more real and vivid. The reality of spiritual warfare is that we must protect our souls from despair that negates our hope in Jesus Christ.

The Devil wants to convince us that there is no hope in life and even less hope in a loving God. Despair is a powerful weapon the Devil continually employs. It's a very simple tool that allows the Devil to manipulate our thoughts, convincing us that God is too far out of reach for us to know, understand, and love. Despair makes a relationship with God seem unattainable. Screwtape aims for Wormwood to undermine the patient's faith and thus cause him to lose hope of developing Christian virtues, since the aim of any Christian virtue is to bring us into a closer relationship with God.

Screwtape encourages Wormwood to get the patient to embrace a sense of despair as a way to combat hope. He offers the suffering of impending war as one way to feed the patient's despair, presenting redemptive suffering as an illusion.

DEBUNKING SCREWTAPE

Despair is an act of the will by which one decides that there is no hope in God either for salvation or the forgiveness of our sins. Despair contradicts faith in God's loving goodness toward us. Let us remember that our Father in heaven is a merciful God. He gave us His only begotten son, Jesus Christ, to save us from the pain of sin and death.

God's mercy has no limit, and thankfully, he can triumph even over our despair. Just because we may not see the hope in the midst of confusion and darkness, we can still discover it later. Ultimately, even in the face of terrible suffering, we can offer our sufferings in union with Christ's sufferings for the redemption of mankind. This is why Screwtape warns Wormwood not to rely too heavily on war to lead the patient into despair, for war can also inspire the heroic virtue of sacrifice.

The sin of despair only tempts us when we think there is nothing to offer us hope. Our Lord continually makes his presence known to us because we are his children. Why wouldn't he want to communicate with us and provide us with the opportunity to be in his presence in heaven? His very existence gives us hope (see CCC 2086), and he has demonstrated through the death of his Son Jesus Christ that he does not want us to stray from him. God always intends to reveal his glory; we can trust this, even when we don't see it.

APPLICATION OF THE *CATECHISM*

The *Catechism* teaches us that a sound way to combat the sin of despair is to follow the first commandment, to love God our Father in heaven above any other god. This act of love serves as a pillar to bolster the virtue of hope and as an antidote to despair. Instead of the continual confusion offered by the Devil, "hope is the confident expectation of divine blessing and the beatific vision of God" (2090).

God is our eternal hope. He is the answer to the sin of despair because he revealed his love for us through his Son Jesus Christ. The opportunity to worship God our Father in heaven awaits us if we keep our hope, trust in him, and do not despair. Prayer is the gateway to hope because it opens the opportunity to be in a mutually active conversation with God. The virtue of hope allows us to remain steadfast in our trust in God. To place our hope in God requires a daily surrender of the will, resting all our hope in him.

The first commandment serves as a gateway toward prayer and establishing a loving relationship with God. In and through the Son of God, despair is destroyed on the cross, and hope reigns. The *Catechism* reminds us:

> The Son of God who, came down "from heaven, not to do [his] own will, but the will of him who sent [him]," said on coming into the world, "Lo, I have come to do your will, O God." "And by that will we have been sanctified through the offering of the body of Jesus Christ once for all." From the first moment of his Incarnation the Son embraces the Father's plan of divine salvation in his redemptive mission: "My food is to do the will of him who sent me, and to accomplish his work." (606)

DISCUSSION QUESTIONS

- How does the sin of despair distract us from loving God?
- How does the virtue of hope help us to understand our salvation with God?
- In what way can the first commandment help us understand God's love?

• • • • •

MEDITATION

(Hebrews 10:23–25)

> Let us hold fast the confession of our hope without wavering, for he who promised is faithful; and let us consider how to stir up one another to love and good works, not neglecting to meet together, as is the habit of some, but encouraging one another, and all the more as you see the Day drawing near.

Chapter 6

Fear of the Lord

And in the fourth watch of the night he came to them, walking on the sea. But when the disciples saw him walking on the sea, they were terrified, saying, "It is a ghost!" And they cried out for fear. But immediately he spoke to them, saying, "Take heart, it is I; have no fear."

— *Matthew 14:25–27*

Your patient will, of course, have picked up the notion that he must submit with patience to the Enemy's will. What the Enemy means by this is primarily that he should accept with patience the tribulation which has actually been dealt out to him — the present anxiety and suspense. It is about this *that he is to say "Thy will be done," and for the daily task of bearing* this *that the daily bread will be provided. It is your business to see that the patient never thinks of the present fear as his appointed cross, but only of the things he is afraid of. ... And let him try to practice fortitude and patience to them all in advance.*

The Screwtape Letters, 6

In his sixth letter, Screwtape encourages Wormwood to keep the patient away from the Enemy (God) by preoccupying him with moments of anxiety and the many fears that naturally arise at the outset of a war. Screwtape charges Wormwood to keep the patient from exercising the virtue of patience, which would serve as a path to his developing an active relationship with God.

Screwtape wants the patient to focus his attention on everything that he is afraid of. Wormwood must teach the patient to try to combat fear as an abstract state of mind rather than facing its real, concrete sources. By fighting the wrong battle, he will learn to develop a cynical view of God, since it will seem that following God's will produces no result. Screwtape wants to manipulate the patient's understanding of what it means to carry his cross for God. Succumbing to fear is a greater cross than following God's commands and facing difficult situations directly.

The patient's fear of anything but God himself leaves the door open to temptation. If the patient shoulders all his burdens himself instead of offering them to God and asking for help through prayer, then he will not see God as a source of grace or healing. By focusing on the things he fears, he becomes disassociated from God.

DEBUNKING SCREWTAPE

Why would anyone want to endure suffering? It's natural to want to avoid any form of suffering because we are human beings, and we desire both physical and spiritual well-being. We naturally avoid occasions of suffering, and the mere thought of embracing pain would make anyone shiver with fear. The Devil twists this natural inclination to avoid suffering into part of his diabolical scheme. He does not want us to view suffering through the lens of Jesus Christ and what he endured on the cross. When he died for our sins, Jesus revealed that suffering has a redemptive nature. Any occasion of suffering provides us with an opportunity to direct both our pain and our souls toward Jesus himself. When a burden becomes too much to handle, what should be our first inclination? Should we ask God to take it away or to give us the strength to bear it?

Jesus set the example by freely choosing to die to conquer sin and death. We have been released from sin and death through the Crucified Lord. The Devil does not want us to understand or embrace this truth. But when we remain centered on Christ, we can learn to see our burdens not as impossible challenges but as pathways through which we recognize God's love for us through his Son.

Saint Peter provides us with a blueprint for directing our burdens and fears to God: "You know that you were ransomed from the futile ways inherited from your fathers, not with perishable things such as silver or gold, but with the precious blood of Christ, like that of a lamb without blemish or spot. He was destined before the foundation of the world but was made manifest at the end of the times for your sake" (1 Pt 1:18–20).

Peter is reminding us that our relationship with Jesus requires us to embrace Our Lord's sacrifice on the cross and be willing to carry our own cross in his name. Bearing our cross in the name of Jesus Christ dispels any unholy fear.

Nothing is impossible if we offer our burdens and fears to God. He expects us to turn to him because he is our Father, and we are his children. He made us in his image and likeness out of love. Fear of the Lord is a gift of the Holy Spirit by which we fully recognize the power and authority of God as all-powerful and all-knowing. It helps us to show awe and reverence to God, to be faithful, and to acknowledge God's presence in our lives. This is the kind of fear that the Devil does not want us to experience because unholy fear is immediately destroyed when we place our trust in God.

APPLICATION OF THE *CATECHISM*

Jesus came to do the will of the Father (CCC 606). He intended to free us from the suffering of sin and death. The *Catechism* reminds us that Jesus Christ came to carry the burdens and sins of humanity and to direct our focus back to the Father. When we experience hardship, our human inclination is to avoid it. Because we have a tendency to seek the path of least resistance and not embrace the cross of Jesus Christ, we easily forget that God the Father offered his only Son to carry our burdens, fears, and sins.

The *Catechism* reminds us that "the cross is the unique sacrifice of Christ, the 'one mediator between God and men.' ... He calls his disciples to 'take up [their] cross and follow [him]'" (618). It is important to understand that our own will should reflect the will of God the Father. What this means is that our life is meant to imitate the life of Jesus Christ, the Son of God. This is accomplished through a sincere effort in prayer, fasting, and sacrifice in the name of Jesus Christ. Jesus reminds us that the way to conquer fear and death is by taking up our cross and following him in hope to our eternal home in heaven.

DISCUSSION QUESTIONS

- How can the fear of the Lord help me understand God's love for me? How can it help dispel unholy fear when it arises in my life?
- How can I offer my burdens and fears to God?
- Why should I fear God? How can fear of the Lord be considered holy?

• • • • •

MEDITATION

(Attributed to St. Rose of Lima)

> Apart from the cross, there is no other ladder by which we may get to heaven.

Chapter 7
Be Wary of the Gift of Ignorance

Be sober, be watchful. Your adversary the devil prowls around like a roaring lion, seeking some one to devour.

— 1 Peter 5:8

> *I wonder you should ask me whether it is essential to keep the patient in ignorance of your own existence. ... Our policy, for the moment, is to conceal ourselves. ... All extremes, except extreme devotion to the Enemy, are to be encouraged. ... We want the Church to be small not only that fewer men may know the Enemy but also that those who do may acquire the uneasy intensity and the defensive self-righteousness of a secret society or a clique.*
>
> The Screwtape Letters, 7

In chapter seven, we encounter Screwtape encouraging Wormwood to keep the patient ignorant of his own identity. He does not want the patient to know that the Devil exists or that his legions have any influence on humanity.

Screwtape instructs Wormwood to be silent but present to the patient. The aim is to keep the patient engaged with the calamities of the world while preventing him from recognizing the Devil's presence. At the same time, Screwtape encourages Wormwood to keep the patient at a distance from the Enemy and his Church. Even better, he should help the patient create or join factions within the Church that will keep him confused and direct his focus toward the factions themselves rather than toward God.

If Wormwood can get the patient caught up in factions, he can keep the patient from embracing true Christianity, opening up the possibility of tempting him away from his Christian community and his belief in God altogether.

DEBUNKING SCREWTAPE

The Church will continue to exist, whether the Devil reveals himself or not. His attempt to keep us ignorant of his existence can only last as long as the Devil himself hides his need to prowl around the world, seeking to ruin our souls. Because the Devil's appetite for the destruction of souls through all forms of sinful temptation is insatiable, he will eventually make his presence known.

When something distracts us from God, it is important to investigate the source of the distraction. We must be willing to ask ourselves why we are choosing this distraction over building our relationship with Christ.

APPLICATION OF THE *CATECHISM*

God is the divine pedagogue, which means that he is the master, teacher, and communicator of his own Word to us. He wants to be in constant contact with us, and he wants us to believe that he does not abandon us. God never stops seeking to develop an intimate relationship with us. We are part of God's kingdom; we are all called to enter the kingdom (see CCC 543). Saint Paul reminds us that God's "'grace is sufficient for you, for [His] power is made perfect in weakness.' I will all the more gladly boast of my weaknesses, that the power of Christ may rest upon me. For the sake of Christ, then, I am content with weaknesses, insults, hardships, persecutions, and calamities; for when I am weak, then I am strong" (2 Cor 12:9–10).

Through baptism, we are united with God the Father, God the Son, and God the Holy Spirit. The Church established by Christ on earth is the authentic representation of unity between us and God. If the Devil can attack our unified bond of faith with one another, he can deeply wound our relationship with God as well. The *Catechism* reminds us:

> *The Church is one because of her source*: "the highest exemplar and source of this mystery is the unity, in the Trinity of Persons, of one God, the Father and the Son in the Holy Spirit." The Church is one *because of her founder*: for "the Word made flesh, the prince of peace, reconciled all men to God by the cross, ... restoring the unity of all in one people and one body." The Church is one *because of her "soul"*: "It is the Holy Spirit, dwelling in those who believe and pervading and ruling over the entire Church, who brings about that wonderful communion of the faithful and joins them together so intimately in Christ that he is the principle of the Church's unity." Unity is of the essence of the Church. (813)

Awareness of God also requires an awareness of the antithesis of God, who is the Devil. The Church serves as our sanctuary to pray to and worship God through his Son Jesus Christ, who also revealed to us the nature of the Devil when he resisted his temptations in the desert (see Mt 4:1–11).

DISCUSSION QUESTIONS

- God gave us a Church through which to pray and worship him. How can the Church help me grow in my relationship with God?
- How does the virtue of hope help us recognize that a spiritual battle between good and evil exists?
- How can we better recognize the presence of both God and the Devil in our lives?

• • • • •

MEDITATION

(St. Charles de Foucauld)

> Father, I abandon myself into your hands;
> do with me what you will.
> Whatever you may do, I thank you:
> I am ready for all, I accept all.

Chapter 8
Bad Habits

And you he made alive, when you were dead through the trespasses and sins in which you once walked, following the course of this world, following the prince of the power of the air, the spirit that is now at work in the sons of disobedience.

— *Ephesians 2:1–2*

> *Humans are amphibians — half spirit and half animal. ... As spirits, they belong to the eternal world, but as animals they inhabit time. This means that while their spirit can be directed to an eternal object, their bodies, passions, and imaginations are in continual change, for to be in time means to change. Their nearest approach to constancy, therefore, is undulation — the repeated return to a level from which they repeatedly fall back, a series of troughs and peaks.*
>
> The Screwtape Letters, 8

In chapter eight, we encounter a very cautious Screwtape who is wary of assuming that the patient's religious habits will simply fade away because he is in a spiritual "trough" or low period. Screwtape cautions Wormwood not to assume that the patient will stop being religious and fall into his tempting hands simply because he has hit a "trough" in his spiritual life.

Screwtape warns Wormwood that God wants the patient to learn how to seek God on his own through the various challenges of life, and to continue to live his faith even when he doesn't feel it. God desires us to seek him and see him even when we do not want to. Our struggles can strengthen our relationship with God, and that is what he wants for us.

DEBUNKING SCREWTAPE

Being human means facing constant fluctuation and tension. To continue to live the Christian life and do God's will in the face of these changes, we must form consistent habits. The term *habit* often evokes a negative connotation. However, all of us possess both good and bad habits; the question becomes how to do away with the bad and reinforce the good. A spiritual habit created within a proper moral framework can offer a sense of renewal, freedom, and conversion because it is ordered toward Jesus Christ. These good habits help us renounce any evil habits that may tempt us to walk away from God's love, especially in periods of spiritual dryness.

All of us possess the ability to exercise our own free will for good or evil. The gift of freedom "is the power, rooted in reason and will, to act or not to act, to do this or that, and so to perform deliberate actions on one's own responsibility" (CCC 1731). "Freedom makes man *responsible* for his acts to the extent that they are voluntary. Progress in virtue, knowledge of the good, and ascesis [the practice of penance, mortification, and self-denial] enhance the mastery of the will over its acts" (1734).

Our free will is a gift from God, and it is meant ultimately to be conformed to God's will. The key to conforming our will to his is developing good moral habits. We can start by placing ourselves before Jesus and telling him directly, "I love you more, Lord, than my own desires." This is the first step toward renouncing sinful habits and embracing good ones.

APPLICATION OF THE *CATECHISM*

The basis of our relationship with God is that we choose to love him even when we don't feel like it. God judges human actions by the fundamental truth that man is a moral subject with the freedom to choose. The *Catechism* reminds us that virtue "is an habitual and firm disposition" to do what is good. "It allows the person not only to perform good acts, but to give the best of himself" to God and neighbor, helping him tend toward the good and be like God (1803). The more we build virtuous habits, the less likely we are to stumble and fall when we don't feel like living out our Christian faith.

Let us also not forget the Lord's Prayer, in which Jesus instructs us to pray for the grace to do the will of the Father: "Thy will be done." This important petition calls us to "discern 'what is the will of God' and obtain the endurance to do it. Jesus teaches us that one enters the kingdom of heaven not by speaking words but by doing 'the will of my Father in heaven'" (Rom 12:2; Mt 7:21; CCC 2826).

To seek the will of God and follow him, the *Catechism* tells us we must persevere in love.

> "Pray constantly … always and for everything giving thanks in the name of our Lord Jesus Christ to God the Father." St. Paul adds, "Pray at all times in the Spirit, with all prayer and supplication. To that end keep alert with all perseverance making supplication for all the saints." For "we have not been commanded to work, to keep watch and to fast constantly, but it has been laid down

> that we are to pray without ceasing." This tireless fervor can come only from love. Against our dullness and laziness, the battle of prayer is that of humble, trusting, and persevering *love*. (2742)

DISCUSSION QUESTIONS

- St. Gregory of Nyssa wrote that the goal of a virtuous life is to become like God. What do you think that he means?
- How does the Lord's Prayer, especially meditating on "Thy will be done," help us overcome sinful habits?

• • • • •

MEDITATION

(Ephesians 4:25–27)

> Therefore, putting away falsehood, let every one speak the truth with his neighbor, for we are members one of another. Be angry but do not sin; do not let the sun go down on your anger, and give no opportunity to the devil.

Chapter 9
Spiritual Dryness, Sexual Temptation, and the Dignity of the Human Person

In their case the god of this world has blinded the minds of the unbelievers, to keep them from seeing the light of the gospel of the glory of Christ, who is the likeness of God.

— *2 Corinthians 4:4*

> *I have always found that the trough periods of the human undulation provide excellent opportunity for all sensual temptations, particularly those of sex. ... Never forget that when we are dealing with any pleasure in its healthy and normal and satisfying form, we are ... on the Enemy's ground. ... It is His invention, not ours. He made the pleasures. ... All we can do is to encourage the humans to take the pleasures which our Enemy has produced, at times, or in ways, or in degrees, which He has forbidden.*
>
> The Screwtape Letters, 9

Screwtape and Wormwood are deliberately attempting to weaken the patient's relationship with God in times when he experiences spiritual dryness. Screwtape is hell-bent on leading the patient away from any form of authentic Christian spirituality with Our Lord, and he encourages Wormwood to attack the patient's inner world which is drab, cold, and empty. They seek to exploit the patient's spiritual weaknesses through sensual temptations, especially those centered on sex.

Screwtape intends to attack the gift of the sexual relationship between husband and wife. Authentic spiritual gratification should come from a relationship with God, but Screwtape and Wormwood hope to tempt the patient to seek spiritual gratification from the flesh instead, creating a spiritual divide between the patient and God.

Still, even though he wants to use it to tempt the patient, the gift of pleasure threatens Screwtape because pleasure is designed to put our focus on God. Screwtape encourages Wormwood to manipulate God's gifts by tempting the patient to seek pleasure in forbidden ways.

DEBUNKING SCREWTAPE

Experiencing spiritual dryness in prayer does not mean that Our Lord is not present, or that we are not able to communicate with him. At any moment, our relationship with Jesus Christ may hit a spiritual roadblock because we encounter a temptation to either ignore or walk away from our relationship with him. Spiritual dryness refers to our difficulty in praying to Jesus and encountering his presence. The more we try to build a relationship with Jesus either through prayer, reception of the sacraments, or the practice of the spiritual or corporal works of mercy, the more these gifts of the Church may appear to be hopeless at certain moments in our life. When we encounter spiritual dryness, we are often tempted to abandon our relationship with Jesus, which leads to the inclination to seek comfort from someone or something other than Jesus himself. Concupiscence — the inclination to sin, whether venial or mortal — is a habit that the Devil wants us to develop. He uses sinful pleasure to tempt us and promote aridity in our prayer life, ultimately leading us to despair.

The Devil strategically places the temptations of the body in our path so that we will ignore our identity as people created in the image and likeness of God. He does this especially when we are facing spiritual dryness. One way the Devil seeks to disrupt our relationship with Christ is by manipulating God's gift of sexuality, offering immoral sexual pleasures to entice us away from Our Lord. We are called, even after the Fall of man, to love and adore God and act according to his will. The pleasures of the world cannot and should not replace God's love for us. The Church in her wisdom guides us toward the virtue of humility, which serves as a weapon against both spiritual dryness and sexual temptation.

The virtue of humility calls us to act in a spirit of poverty, serving others before ourselves. Humility helps us remain centered on Jesus Christ and our identity as disciples called to imitate him and his sacrifice on the cross. Humility teaches us that God is the author of everything good, which includes us. The goodness we possess by our creation is an important gift that we should not ignore.

APPLICATION OF THE *CATECHISM*

The *Catechism* reminds us that the way to handle a distraction in prayer is to gradually turn our hearts back to God. We are God's children created out of divine love; thus, we can return to his love and accept it even when we sense that our prayer life is dry or empty. The "humble awareness" of our distraction "should awaken our preferential love for [God] and lead us resolutely to offer him our heart to be purified" (2729):

> Dryness belongs to contemplative prayer when the heart is separated from God, with no taste for thoughts, memories, and feelings, even spiritual ones. This is the moment of sheer faith clinging faithfully to Jesus in his agony and in his tomb. "Unless a grain of wheat falls into the earth and dies, it remains alone; but if it dies, it bears much fruit." If dryness is due to the lack of roots, because the word has fallen on rocky soil, the battle requires conversion. (2731)

The conversion that the *Catechism* speaks of is a conversion toward Christ. It begins at baptism, where the grace of the first sacrament of initiation welcomes us into the kingdom of God with open arms and sets the stage for us to live out our identity as children of God if we so choose.

As challenging as spiritual dryness can be, sexual temptation is often even more daunting because it involves our own bodies which God gave us out of love. The first order of genuine Christian intimacy is to avoid all lustful desires that contradict the gift of human sexuality, which is properly expressed between man and woman through the Sacrament of Holy Matrimony. Let's not forget that sexual intercourse is an act solely reserved for the intimate union of man and woman in marriage. It is "a mutual giving of two persons, and the good of the children, [which demands] total fidelity from the spouses" (1646).

No one is immune from temptation due to sin. All of us struggle with particular sins, some more than others. When we suffer bouts of spiritual dryness, these particular sins can overwhelm us and make us frustrated with ourselves for not being able to withstand temptation. However, understanding the nature of why we engage in this type of sinful behavior allows us to seek the help of Jesus Christ and proclaim our love for him more than our sins. The first step to avoid temptation is to calmly renounce and reject this sin in Jesus' name.

God does not abandon us; instead, he continues to seek an intimate relationship with us as revealed through his Son Jesus Christ. Sin does not define us. God does, because we are his children.

DISCUSSION QUESTIONS

- How can I begin to understand God's love for me?
- Why can't I always see God's love for me?
- How can I prepare myself to face temptations, especially when I'm in periods of spiritual dryness?

• • • • •

MEDITATION

(Romans 12:1–2)

> I appeal to you therefore, brethren, by the mercies of God, to present your bodies as a living sacrifice, holy and acceptable to God, which is your spiritual worship. Do not be conformed to this world but be transformed by the renewal of your mind, that you may prove what is the will of God, what is good and acceptable and perfect.

Chapter 10
A Well-Informed Conscience

So they are without excuse; for although they knew God they did not honor him as God or give thanks to him, but they became futile in their thinking and their senseless minds were darkened.

— *Romans 1:20–21*

> *I gather that the middle-aged married couple who called at his office are just the sort of people we want him to know — rich, smart, superficially intellectual, and brightly skeptical about everything in the world. ... No doubt he must very soon realize that his own faith is in direct opposition to the assumptions on which all the conversation of his new friends is based. ... Persuade him to postpone any open acknowledgment of the fact. ... As long as the postponement lasts, he will be in a false position. He will be silent when he ought to speak and laugh when he ought to be silent. He will assume ... all sorts of cynical and skeptical attitudes which are not really his.*
>
> The Screwtape Letters, 10

It is important to be spiritually vigilant about our acquaintances and friends. We are engaged in a daily battle between good and evil, and remaining vigilant in our relationships protects us from being influenced by our friends' ideas or actions that may lead us away from our relationship with God.

If we surround ourselves with people who exhibit positive moral virtues, we often acquire the habits of those virtues ourselves. Likewise, surrounding ourselves with bad influences can have the opposite effect. Screwtape encourages Wormwood to present the patient with questionable characters who will lead him away from God. Any negative, cynical behavior that the patient's friends exhibit in his presence is a win for Screwtape because the patient will learn to imitate it, and thus drive a spiritual wedge between himself and God. Screwtape wants the patient to find his friends' cynicism more appealing than a Christian worldview.

Screwtape tells Wormwood to inundate the patient with shame and pride to cast a cloud of confusion around how he should behave around his friends. By keeping the patient in a state of moral confusion, the demons hope that he will not realize that his newfound pleasures are really temptations that Christians have preached against for over two thousand years. Screwtape wants to take advantage of the patient's ill-formed moral conscience, and he tells Wormwood to be aware that the patient may eventually realize that he has not chosen his friends very well. Yet if he still feels attached to them, he can be convinced to live a double life.

DEBUNKING SCREWTAPE

Every day, we make decisions that affect ourselves and those around us. Whether or not the decisions are based on a properly formed moral conscience, our actions have consequences. The people we choose to develop a relationship with (or even more, to count among our friends) strongly influence how we view the world, our relationship with God, and how we fit within God's plan for salvation. If our conscience is well-formed, leading us to imitate Christ and faithfully live out our faith, then we will typically seek friendships that support these good intentions. We fall into danger when we engage in relationships that tempt us to avoid God, even in small, subtle ways.

True friendship is not rooted in man, but in man's relationship with Jesus Christ. Jesus provides us with the grace to make right moral judgments and develop a well-informed moral conscience. Screwtape underestimates man's ability to seek good amidst a world of evil, for man has in his heart a law inscribed by God (see CCC 1776).

APPLICATION OF THE *CATECHISM*

The *Catechism* reminds us that moral conscience is "present at the heart" of every person. It engages us "at the appropriate moment" to prompt us "to do good and to avoid evil" (1777). It goes on:

> Conscience is a judgment of reason whereby the human person recognizes the moral quality of a concrete act that he is going to perform, is in the process of performing, or has already completed. In all he says and does, man is obliged to follow faithfully what he knows to be just and right. It is by the judgment of his conscience that man perceives and recognizes the prescriptions of the divine law. (1778)

St. John Henry Newman describes the gift of conscience as "a law of the mind. … [Conscience] is a messenger of him, who, both in nature and in grace, speaks to us behind a veil, and teaches and rules us by his representatives. Conscience is the aboriginal Vicar of Christ" (1778). A well-formed moral conscience recognizes the dignity of another human being. Hence, we identify with one another as children of God to be respected and loved in the name of Our Lord Jesus Christ. "The dignity of a human person implies and requires *uprightness of moral conscience*" (1780).

The *Catechism* reminds us that a properly informed moral conscience helps us:

- perform good works and avoid evil ones
- judge the particular choices we make
- recognize the authority of truth
- welcome the commandments
- hear God speak

Saint Augustine wrote, "Return to your conscience, question it. ... Turn inward, brethren, and in everything you do, see God as your witness" (1779).

DISCUSSION QUESTIONS

- › How does an active relationship with Jesus Christ help me develop a sound moral conscience?
- › Why is the development of a properly formed conscience important in the development of genuine friendships? How does our conscience help us avoid negative and sinful influences from our friends?
- › Why are the Ten Commandments important in developing a proper moral conscience?
- › How does the Gospel story about Jesus in the desert help us understand the importance of trusting in God through our most challenging times?

• • • • •

MEDITATION

(Romans 2:14–16)

> When Gentiles who have not the law do by nature what the law requires, they are a law to themselves, even though they do not have the law. They show that what the law requires is written on their hearts, while their conscience also bears witness and their conflicting thoughts accuse or perhaps excuse them on that day when, according to my gospel, God judges the secrets of men by Christ Jesus.

Chapter 11
A Perversion of Joy

Whatever is true, whatever is honorable, whatever is just, whatever is pure, whatever is lovely, whatever is gracious, if there is any excellence, if there is anything worthy of praise, think about these things.

— *Philippians 4:8*

> *I divide the causes of human laughter into Joy, Fun, the Joke Proper, and Flippancy. You will see the first among friends and lovers reunited on the eve of a holiday. ... Something like this is expressed in much of that detestable art which the humans call Music, and something like it occurs in Heaven. ... Laughter of this kind does us no good and should always be discouraged. ... Fun is closely related to Joy. ... It is very little use to us. The Joke Proper ... is a much more promising field.*
>
> The Screwtape Letters, 11

In chapter eleven, Screwtape references four types of human laughter: joy, fun, the joke proper, and flippancy. Screwtape views only two of these categories of laughter as opportunities to guide the patient to act in a way contrary to Christian virtue. The Joke Proper serves as an opportunity to trivialize lust and sex, allowing the patient to discuss sex in an unholy way that his friends will approve. Flippancy works much the same way; sarcasm that demeans another person but elicits laughter is socially acceptable in a way that serious insults are not. By encouraging the patient to view these behaviors in a comical way, Screwtape and Wormwood can break down his sense of shame. Screwtape summarizes his mission thus: "Cruelty is shameful — unless the cruel man can represent it as a practical joke."

DEBUNKING SCREWTAPE

All of us bear the image and likeness of God. He created us in his image and likeness out of love. It is important to understand the gift of our identity as God's children because the Devil would prefer that we devalue ourselves under the guise of jokes and flippancy. The Devil aims to devalue all virtues, but through the improper use of humor, he takes special care to pervert joy. Joy is one of the fruits of the Holy Spirit, which "are perfections that the Holy Spirit forms in us as the first fruits of eternal glory" (CCC 1832). Targeting the patient's joy is a direct attack on his identity as a child of God led and nurtured by the Spirit. By subverting the actions of the Holy Spirit, Screwtape can damage the patient's ability to grow in virtue.

APPLICATION OF THE *CATECHISM*

The *Catechism* teaches us that "a virtue is an habitual and firm disposition to do the good. It allows the person not only to perform good acts, but to give the best of himself. The virtuous person tends toward the good with all his sensory and spiritual powers; he pursues the good and chooses it in concrete actions. 'The goal of a virtuous life is to become like God'" (1803).

The *Catechism* goes on to describe human virtues as "firm attitudes, stable dispositions, habitual perfections of intellect and will that govern our actions, order our passions, and guide our conduct according to reason and faith. They make possible ease, self-mastery, and joy in leading a morally good life. The virtuous man is he who freely practices the good" (1804).

It is important that we maintain an active and loving relationship with Jesus Christ because exercising any virtue requires human effort. The three theological virtues — faith, hope, and love — establish a foundation for living a virtuous life centered on the Trinity because it is through the Trinity that we receive our identity as Christians at baptism. The cardinal virtues, especially the virtue of prudence, serve as a spiritual gauge that helps us differentiate virtue from vice. The cardinal virtues are acquired by education, deliberate acts, and perseverance. However, it is important to remember that they are also "purified and elevated by divine grace" (1810). Therefore, we must also acquire them through prayer. Pray for the virtue of *prudence* to provide practical wisdom and spiritual insight to make right choices (see 1 Pt 4:7). Pray for the virtue of *justice* to respect both God and neighbor (Lv 19:15). Pray for the virtue of *fortitude* to be firm in pursuing good and overcoming evil (Ps 118:14). Pray for the virtue of *temperance* to moderate attractions and worldly pleasures.

The cardinal virtues lead us to genuine joy as part of our relationship with Jesus Christ. Joy, as a fruit of the Spirit, helps us to renounce ourselves as we grow in our relationship with Jesus Christ. The more we live a virtuous life, the more we experience the gift of joy.

DISCUSSION QUESTIONS

› How can someone live a virtuous life with sin in his heart? Is confession the first step toward starting a virtuous relationship with Jesus Christ?

- How can the cardinal virtues help us in our struggle to pray to God?
- Why is joy synonymous with having a relationship with Jesus Christ? In what ways do we pervert the gift of joy?

• • • • •

MEDITATION

(Romans 8:14, 17)

> For all who are led by the Spirit of God are sons of God. And if children, then heirs, heirs of God and fellow heirs with Christ.

Chapter 12
The Great Deception

If we say we have no sin, we deceive ourselves, and the truth is not in us.

— 1 John 1:8

> *As long as he retains externally the habits of a Christian he can still be made to think of himself as one who has adopted a few new friends and amusements but whose spiritual state is much the same as it was six weeks ago. ... As the uneasiness and his reluctance to face it cuts him off more and more from all real happiness, and as habit renders the pleasures of vanity and excitement and flippancy at once less pleasant and harder to forgo ... you will find that anything or nothing is sufficient to attract his wandering attention.*
>
> The Screwtape Letters, 12

In this chapter, Screwtape wants Wormwood to encourage the patient to become spiritually complacent. Complacency encourages us to drift away from the Church and presents the false notion that there is no need to investigate the dangers of sin or the love of Jesus Christ in our lives. If the patient keeps up the outward habits of a Christian while surrounding himself with temptations, he can be made to think that his spiritual state is much the same as it was before. He can fall casually into sin without even realizing that he has done so.

There is a difference between praying to intercede on behalf of someone in need and praying simply to fulfill an obligation. One action is sacrificial in nature, while the other is self-serving. If we maintain a pretense of prayer while actively putting ourselves into the path of temptation, then our actions do not strive for holiness. True prayer requires a firm commitment to amend our lives for the sake of true conversion.

The Devil wants to perpetuate the great deception by which we convince ourselves that we do not sin, or that our sins are not truly problematic.

DEBUNKING SCREWTAPE

Saint Paul, the great apostle to the Gentiles, reminds us of the temptation to fool ourselves in our prayer and devotion to Jesus Christ: "Let no one deceive himself. If any one among you thinks that he is wise in this age, let him become a fool that he may become wise. For the wisdom of this world is folly with God. For it is written, 'He catches the wise in their craftiness'" (1 Cor 3:18–19).

Screwtape coaches Wormwood to encourage the patient to embrace the world and all its empty promises that will guide him away from the Church. Though the Devil's deception strikes at the core of man's sinfulness, it cannot destroy moral truth. Why? Man's soul is ordered toward the good because it is created by God. When sin enters the heart of man, however, he becomes engaged in a battle between good and evil.

What Screwtape describes as the patient's uneasiness is really a battle between good and evil in his soul. Repentance is always right around the corner if he attends to the voice of his conscience. This is why Screwtape encourages Wormwood to "attract his wandering attention" away from the voice of conscience and repentance.

Screwtape is content to let the patient go to church on Sunday as long as he views it as simply another meeting or a gathering of people to pray. He encourages the patient to think that there is nothing spiritually significant about this activity; if the Devil can convince us that religious exercises are meaningless, he can make us fall into his hand. But as Catholics, we must never underestimate the power of the Eucharist, in which "the soul is filled with grace and a pledge of the life to come is given to us" (CCC 1402). As long as we continue to receive, God will use the sacrament to call us to conversion and fill us "with every grace and heavenly blessing" (1402).

APPLICATION OF THE *CATECHISM*

The definition of sin, according to the *Catechism*, is "an offense against reason, truth, and right conscience; it is failure in genuine love for God and neighbor caused by a perverse attachment to certain goods. ... It has been defined as 'an utterance, a deed, or a desire contrary to the eternal law'" (1849). The *Catechism* also reminds us that sin is a failure to obey the two greatest commandments, to love Our Lord and to love our brothers and sisters (1849–1850).

Our duty as Christians is to meditate on the passion of the Son of God, Jesus Christ, and then imitate his self-sacrifice by avoiding the near occasion of sin. The passion also reveals the violent nature of sin. Once we recognize what sin really is and how it can affect our lives, we learn the truth and thus thwart the Devil's great deception. Once we see the truth of our sinfulness, "the sacrifice of Christ ... becomes the source from which the forgiveness of our sins will pour forth inexhaustibly" (1851).

DISCUSSION QUESTIONS

- How does sin disrupt my relationship with Jesus Christ?
- How do I recognize my own sinful behaviors?
- Once recognized, how should I address them?

• • • • •

MEDITATION

(Examining One's Conscience — 1 John 3:19–24)

> By this we shall know that we are of the truth, and reassure our hearts before him whenever our hearts condemn us; for God is greater than our hearts, and he knows everything. Beloved, if our hearts do not condemn us, we have confidence before God; and we receive from him whatever we ask, because we keep his commandments and do what pleases him. And this is his commandment, that we should believe in the name of his Son Jesus Christ and love one another, just as he has commanded us. All who keep his commandments abide in him, and he in them. And by this we know that he abides in us, by the Spirit which he has given us.

Chapter 13
Truth, Beauty, and Goodness

The true light that enlightens every man
was coming into the world.

— *John 1:9*

You have let the man slip through your fingers. ... A repentance and renewal of what the other side call "grace" on the scale which you describe is a defeat of the first order. It amounts to a second conversion. ... You first of all allowed the patient to read a book he really enjoyed, because he enjoyed it and not in order to make clever remarks about it to his new friends. In the second place, you allowed him to walk down to the old mill and have tea there — a walk through the country he really likes, and taken alone. In other words, you allowed him two real positive Pleasures. ... The characteristic of Pains and Pleasures is that they are unmistakably real, and ... give the man who feels them a touchstone of reality.

The Screwtape Letters, 13

Screwtape scolds Wormwood for allowing the patient to enjoy a good book and a walk to have tea. He fears allowing the patient to experience positive pleasures, or in other words, truth, beauty, and goodness. According to Screwtape, these positive experiences will enable the patient to detach from himself and devote his life to the Enemy — God.

DEBUNKING SCREWTAPE

Because of our fallen condition, we are easily susceptible to a multitude of sins. One of these sins is to disregard that God made us out of love. We are not responsible for our own creation but merely cooperators in the gift of life. Because we are created by God, who is Truth, Beauty, and Goodness, we are also created to gravitate toward things of this earth that are true, beautiful, and good. These three characteristics reflect the Trinity, in which we see the revelation of God's love for us through Jesus Christ, the Son of God, and the Holy Spirit, who is the breath and voice of God.

The incarnate Son of God, Jesus Christ, is the fulfillment of truth, beauty, and goodness because he is the Word-made-flesh, both fully human and fully divine, who revealed himself to us so that we may know God more intimately. When we surrender to natural truth, beauty, and goodness, we affirm our devotion to God, which can help us walk away from temptation. The more we recognize that these three characteristics — truth, beauty, and goodness — come from God, the more we will see these gifts in each human being we encounter because each is made by God.

The Devil does not want us to give credence to God in any way, especially by recognizing him in the created universe and its inhabitants. If the Devil can keep us miserable and maintain our focus on ourselves, then we may never encounter the divine gifts Our Lord has created for us.

APPLICATION OF THE *CATECHISM*

The *Catechism* reminds us that we are created to walk toward truth. When God asked Adam and Eve what they had done after they ate from the tree in the Garden, Adam and Eve chose to lie. The battle against truth began with the first sinful act against God. Yet "man tends by nature toward the truth. He is obliged to honor and bear witness to it" (2467), and this is still true of us even though we are now weakened by sin.

Keep in mind that the Devil wants to pervert our minds by encouraging us to seek the opposite of truth, beauty, and goodness. For example, he entices us toward pornography and lust rather than toward the true expression of our sexuality within marriage; toward envy and jealousy rather than the love that celebrates our neighbors. We must aim to avoid the attachments of the world that contradict truth, beauty, and goodness.

DISCUSSION QUESTIONS

- How can I rediscover the goodness of God's creation?
- How does a walk in a park or a hike through a forest help me appreciate the gifts of God's creation?
- In what way can having a fruitful conversation with someone help me understand my relationship with God?

• • • • •

MEDITATION

(Wisdom 13:3)

> If through delight in the beauty of these things men
> assumed them to be gods,
> let them know how much better than these is their
> Lord,
> for the author of beauty created them.

Chapter 14
Humble Yourself

Humble yourselves therefore under the mighty hand of God, that in due time he may exalt you.

— *1 Peter 5:6*

> *Your patient has become humble; have you drawn his attention to the fact? All virtues are less formidable to us once the man is aware that he has them, but this is especially true of humility. Catch him at the moment when he is really poor in spirit and smuggle into his mind the gratifying reflection, "By jove! I'm being humble," and almost immediately pride — pride at his own humility — will appear.*
>
> The Screwtape Letters, 14

Humility strikes at the heart of Screwtape, and the patient has unfortunately developed a sense of humility. The prevailing theme of chapter fourteen is Screwtape's lust to rid the patient of all true humility. He would prefer the patient congratulate himself on being humble rather than exercise the gift of true humility that will bring him closer to God. Screwtape wants to make sure that the patient turns his attention to himself rather than God, thus negating the virtue of humility altogether.

DEBUNKING SCREWTAPE

The virtue of humility can be defined as possessing poverty in spirit, which acknowledges that God is the author of life and everything that is good. It also serves as the foundation of prayer. Humility leads us toward sacrifice, denial of worldly pleasures, and admitting when we are wrong. The virtue of humility guides us to acts of self-abandonment and allows us to emphasize the needs of others before our own. It directs our attention to God before ourselves, which encourages us to serve rather than be served. Through humble self-surrender to God the Father, we acknowledge that we are nothing without God. The gift of humility destroys the sin of pride that aims to take away our relationship with God.

APPLICATION OF THE *CATECHISM*

The *Catechism* reminds us that we are called to poverty of spirit (see 2546). This means that our daily walk with God should begin with the submission of our hearts to him as we acknowledge him as our Father in heaven. In the Gospel of Saint Luke, Jesus reminds the apostles that the cost of discipleship is to renounce all that they have (see 14:33).

"All Christ's faithful are to 'direct their affections rightly, lest they be hindered in their pursuit of perfect charity by the use of worldly things … which is contrary to the spirit of evangelical poverty" (CCC 2545). We should never place ourselves above anyone and should direct our actions toward helping those in need, especially the poor, while recognizing the awesome power of God and his goodness revealed through his Son Jesus Christ. In a practical way, we can confront the sin of pride and grow in humility by living the Beatitudes each day (see Mt 5:3–12).

As St. Gregory of Nyssa said, "The world speaks of voluntary humility as poverty in spirit; the Apostle gives an example of God's poverty when he says, for your sakes he became poor."

DISCUSSION QUESTIONS

- Should I pray for humility? Why?
- Why is the virtue of humility necessary to be an effective disciple of Jesus Christ?

• • • • •

MEDITATION

(Litany of Humility)

His Eminence Cardinal Merry del Val was accustomed to reciting this litany daily after he celebrated the Holy Mass.

O Jesus meek and humble of heart, hear me.
From the desire of being esteemed, deliver me, Jesus.
From the desire of being loved, deliver me, Jesus.
From the desire of being extolled, deliver me, Jesus.
From the desire of being honored, deliver me, Jesus.
From the desire of being praised, deliver me, Jesus.
From the desire of being preferred, deliver me, Jesus.
From the desire of being consulted, deliver me, Jesus.
From the desire of being approved, deliver me, Jesus.
From the fear of being humiliated, deliver me, Jesus.
From the fear of being despised, deliver me, Jesus.
From the fear of suffering rebukes, deliver me, Jesus.
From the fear of being calumniated, deliver me, Jesus.
From the fear of being forgotten, deliver me, Jesus.
From the fear of being ridiculed, deliver me, Jesus.

From the fear of being wronged, deliver me, Jesus.
From the fear of being suspected, deliver me, Jesus.
That others may be loved more than I, Jesus, grant me the grace to desire it.
That others may be esteemed more than I, Jesus, grant me the grace to desire it.
That in the opinion of the world others may increase and I may decrease, Jesus, grant me the grace to desire it.
That others may be chosen and I set aside, Jesus, grant me the grace to desire it.
That others may be praised and I unnoticed, Jesus, grant me the grace to desire it.
That others may become holier than I, provided that I may became as holy as I should, Jesus, grant me the grace to desire it.

Chapter 15
Heaven or ... ?

If then you have been raised with Christ, seek the things that are above, where Christ is, seated at the right hand of God. Set your minds on things that are above, not on things that are on earth.

— *Colossians 3:1–2*

> *The humans live in time but our Enemy destines them to eternity. He ... wants them to attend chiefly to two things, to eternity itself, and to that point of time which they call the Present. For the Present is the point at which time touches eternity. ... Our business is to get them away from the eternal, and from the Present. ... It is far better to make them live in the Future. ... The Future is, of all things, the thing* least like *eternity. ... The Past is frozen and no longer flows, and the Present is all lit up with eternal rays. ... Hence nearly all vices are rooted in the future.*
>
> The Screwtape Letters, 15

Screwtape urges Wormwood to distract the patient from living his life as a preparation for heaven. Part of his strategy to lure the patient into hell is to teach him to consume himself with thoughts of the future and how it will affect him. By enticing him to focus on concerns about his earthly future, Wormwood can teach the patient to lose sight of eternity. According to Screwtape, nearly all vices are rooted in man's looking toward the future.

DEBUNKING SCREWTAPE

Living in the present serves as a daily renewal of our relationship with God. Every day, God gives us an opportunity to interact with those around us, to engage in conversation and affirm our identity as children of God living within a community of faith. Our future is dependent on how we live now, and we can use the present to prepare for eternity through prayer, fasting, adoration of the Blessed Sacrament, and active participation at Mass.

The Devil never rests in his attempts to convince man to despair about the sins of the past so that he has no hope for the future. Focusing on our earthly future serves as a good distraction from focusing on heaven. We stem the Devil's influence by thanking Our Lord for giving us another day to praise him and to express our devotion to him. Part of living in the present is taking care of those around us, placing the needs of our brothers and sisters before our own. This is part of living out the commandments to love God and neighbor.

APPLICATION OF THE *CATECHISM*

The *Catechism* reminds us that "'all Christians in any state or walk of life are called to the fullness of Christian life and to the perfection of charity.' All are called to holiness. ... Spiritual progress tends toward ever more intimate union with Christ" (2013–2014). Living in the present moment is intimately tied to the way of the cross because our daily living is rooted in the renunciation of sin and the spiritual battle associated in our relationship with Jesus Christ. God constantly reveals himself to us through the use of our senses, body, heart, and mind. He does this in order to help us understand his love for us and to reciprocate that love to our brothers and sisters in Christ. God desires that we remain close to him in our journey of faith. He brought Jesus into this world to help us know his love through the sacrifice of his Son. The Church serves as the constant reminder of that love in our daily struggle to be in communion with him.

DISCUSSION QUESTIONS

- How can prayer help me stay focused in my daily Christian living?
- How can the Church help me stay focused on my journey to heaven, rather than allowing the future to absorb my attention?

• • • • •

MEDITATION

(1 John 3:1–2)

> See what love the Father has given us, that we should be called children of God; and so we are. The reason why the world does not know us is that it did not know him. Beloved, we are God's children now; it does not yet appear what we shall be, but we know that when he appears we shall be like him, for we shall see him as he is.

Chapter 16
A Church of Convenience

For he has made known to us in all wisdom and insight the mystery of his will, according to his purpose which he set forth in Christ as a plan for the fullness of time, to unite all things in him, things in heaven and things on earth.

— *Ephesians 1:9–10*

If a man can't be cured of churchgoing, the next best thing is to send him all over the neighborhood looking for the church that "suits" him until he becomes a taster or connoisseur of churches. ... The two churches nearest him ... have certain claims. At the first of these the Vicar is a man who has been so long engaged in watering down the faith to make it easier for a supposedly incredulous and hard-headed congregation that it is now he who shocks his parishioners with his unbelief. ... At the other church we have Fr. Spike. ... He is one day almost Communist and the next not far from some kind of theocratic Fascism — one day a scholastic, and the next prepared to deny human reason altogether. ... There is also a promising streak of dishonesty in him. ... But I must warn you that he has one fatal defect: he really believes.

The Screwtape Letters, 16

Screwtape wants Wormwood to keep the patient from attending one particular church, but instead to have him shop around amongst various churches. The act of church shopping will distract the patient from experiencing authentic community and hence a deeper appreciation for God. Screwtape prefers that the patient discover the least faithful environment, and the worst preaching possible, to evoke spiritual frustration and boredom. Screwtape makes specific mention of Fr. Spike, who appears to be spiritually lost, vacillating from one topic to another and offering no sound spiritual counsel. But Fr. Spike has one quality that poses a danger to Screwtape: Despite his politics, he truly believes in God.

DEBUNKING SCREWTAPE

The Church of Jesus Christ is not a house of worldly convenience. Rather, when someone enters the Catholic Church, he enters into a relationship with Jesus Christ and witnesses firsthand what he did for us on the cross. The Devil wants us to view the Church as a convenience store where we pay for the item we desire — sacraments — and then we think none the better of what we received. The way to debunk Screwtape is to ask ourselves why the Church exists and how the Church represents Jesus Christ.

When we enter a Catholic Church, we walk into a mystery that we can understand in relation to what has been revealed by God through his Son Jesus Christ. The priest, who through his ordination acts in the Person of Jesus Christ, proclaims the Word of God in Sacred Scripture and then consecrates bread and wine into the actual Body and Blood of Jesus Christ so that we can participate in Jesus' divine nature. For "the Word became flesh to make us '*partakers of the divine nature*'" (CCC 460).

In the Church, our hearts can be converted to Jesus Christ through the proclamation of the Word and the reception of Jesus' Body and Blood in the Holy Eucharist. This is exactly what the Devil fears the most: our active engagement in the Mass and our resolution to keep attending.

APPLICATION OF THE *CATECHISM*

The Church is a gift from Jesus Christ, which he established through Saint Peter and the apostles (see Mt 16:16–19). The Church is not meant to cater to our personal preferences. It's a good exercise to make an examination of conscience on this point. Ask yourself: Do I find reasons not to attend Mass? Do I stick with one church, or do I shop for a church that meets my preferences?

We may think that our own sins are too great to allow us to step into a Catholic Church, or that our particular parish is boring or out of touch. But the reality is that our baptism calls us to participate in Christ's mission as priest, prophet, and king (CCC 871). We are part of God's community because of our relationship as his children, created in his image and likeness.

We live out our baptismal call in the community of our parish, "the place where all the faithful can be gathered together for the Sunday celebration of the Eucharist. The parish initiates the Christian people into the ordinary expression of the liturgical life: it gathers them together in this celebration; it teaches Christ's saving doctrine; it practices the charity of the Lord in good works and brotherly love" (2179).

DISCUSSION QUESTIONS

- How can I be more committed to and engaged in my parish community?

- How can a community of believers who actively believe in God help me understand my relationship with him?
- How can I enter more fully into the Mass and allow it to strengthen my vocation as a disciple of Jesus Christ?
- Why did Jesus establish a Church on earth? How does she help us grow in our relationship with him?

• • • • •

MEDITATION

(St. John Chrysostom)

> You cannot pray at home as at church, where there is a great multitude, where exclamations are cried out to God as from one great heart, and where there is something more: the union of minds, the accord of souls, the bond of charity, the prayers of the priests.†

† St. John Chrysostom, *De incomprehensibili*, 3, 6, PG 48, 725.

Chapter 17
Self-Mastery

The man said, "The woman whom you gave to be with me, she gave me fruit of the tree, and I ate." Then the Lord God said to the woman, "What is this that you have done?" The woman said, "The serpent beguiled me, and I ate."

— *Genesis 3:12–13*

The contemptuous way in which you spoke of gluttony as a means of catching souls, in your last letter, only shows your ignorance. One of the great achievements of the last hundred years has been to deaden the human conscience on that subject. ... This has largely been effected by concentrating all our efforts on gluttony of Delicacy, not gluttony of Excess. Your patient's mother ... is a good example. She would be astonished ... to learn that her whole life is enslaved to this kind of sensuality, which is quite concealed from her by the fact that the quantities involved are small.

The Screwtape Letters, 17

Habits can be very hard to break, especially if these habits provide us with physical comforts. The danger with these habits is that they can lead us away from a relationship with Jesus Christ, which is, of course, what the Devil prefers. In this chapter, we encounter Screwtape expressing glee at the habitual gluttonous actions of the patient's mother. She is driven by human desires to satisfy her physical urges. These urges affected the mother's actions toward food, or the lack thereof, and appear to have dominated her whole life, even affecting her relationship with her son and those around her.

Screwtape directs Wormwood to use the example of the mother's gluttony to attack the patient through gluttony as a way to lead the patient to be unchaste because he is in the habit of satisfying all his carnal desires.

DEBUNKING SCREWTAPE

Keep in mind that man was created by God in his image and likeness. The Devil cannot claim authorship or ownership over man, which is why he must tempt man to destroy himself from within — he is powerless to do harm without man's consent. Even after Adam and Eve fell by committing the first sin against God, God did not reject them. He cast them out of the Garden of Eden due to their free choice to love their vices more than him, but he still offered them mercy and an opportunity to resuscitate their relationship with him.

Screwtape views the sin of gluttony as a gateway to other sins — in this case, sexual immorality. When our first parents introduced and accepted sin, the desire for lustful carnal pleasures — unchastity — became prevalent and debilitating to both man and woman. Instead of expressing a mutual love of integrity toward one another, they now desired only to fulfill a sexual appetite, thus introducing the sin of sexual gluttony.

Screwtape's aim here is to enslave both the patient's mother and the patient himself with the sin of gluttony. As this sin gradually becomes habitual, we cease to view our bodies as a gift from God. Instead, the body serves the purpose of satisfying our gluttonous cravings. Only when we embrace the way of the cross, the example of Jesus, can we overcome the sin of gluttony.

Our Lord's mercy has no limits, and his love is fully revealed in his death on the cross. His resurrection conquered sin and death. It is important to know that God's love, as revealed through Jesus Christ, is merciful and without limits. God loves his children and does not abandon them; on the contrary, he offered his Son for us. If we extend our hand toward God, he will immediately embrace it because we are his children, and a father is always ready to care for his children.

APPLICATION OF THE *CATECHISM*

The *Catechism* reminds us that, because man is free, if he has not bound himself to the ultimate good, which is God, he can choose to commit evil acts (1732). We also possess the freedom to master our own actions, including the ability to avoid any vice that may wound our relationship with Jesus Christ. Our aim should be to control our sinful urges and selfish desires, and thereby progress toward goodness. Self-mastery reflects a desire to respect oneself, others, and God, and it is essential to combat gluttony. An important virtue to practice to combat gluttony of any kind is *temperance*, which helps us moderate the degree to which we engage in pleasures (1809).

DISCUSSION QUESTIONS

- What practical actions can I take to renounce a sinful habit that continues to bother me?
- How can an examination of conscience help me walk away from my vices?

› Why is the cardinal virtue of temperance important to practice in my daily life?

• • • • •

MEDITATION
(Sirach 37:27–31)

My son, test your soul while you live;
    see what is bad for it and do not give it that.
For not everything is good for every one,
    and not every person enjoys everything.
Do not have an insatiable appetite for any luxury,
    and do not give yourself up to food;
for overeating brings sickness,
    and gluttony leads to nausea.
Many have died of gluttony,
    but he who is careful to avoid it prolongs his life.

Chapter 18
Sex Is a Gift from God

For this is the will of God, your sanctification: that you abstain from immorality; that each one of you know how to control his own body in holiness and honor, not in the passion of lust like heathens who do not know God. … For God has not called us for uncleanness, but in holiness. Therefore whoever disregards this, disregards not man but God, who gives his Holy Spirit to you.

— *1 Thessalonians 4:3–8*

> *The Enemy described a married couple as "one flesh." He did not say "a happily married couple" or "a couple who married because they were in love," but you can make the humans ignore that. … In other words, the humans are to be encouraged to regard as the basis for marriage a highly-colored and distorted version of something the Enemy really promises as its result.*
>
> The Screwtape Letters, 18

Screwtape is openly exasperated with God's view of sex. The thought that love is associated with charity, unity, chastity, sacrifice, and abstinence is foreign to Screwtape. He believes authentic spousal love is an impossibility due to man's lustful desire for sex.

Screwtape defines sex as an act that should have one purpose: satisfying the sexual pleasure of one person at the expense of the other. He seeks to redefine sexual intimacy in a way that divorces it from authentic love. The practices of monogamy and abstinence baffle Screwtape, and he mocks God's position that in the Sacrament of Marriage, a man and a woman become *one flesh*. The Devil prefers to entice people into infidelity by presenting them with a false and unattainable ideal of marriage as constant romantic bliss.

DEBUNKING SCREWTAPE

Sex is a gift; this has been God's intention from the beginning of creation. Adam and Eve were created as perfect physical complements to one another: husband and wife, one flesh. Man, woman, sex, and the virtue of love are inseparable if the couple identifies their union as a mutual gift to one another in accordance with the will of God. This relationship also defines the gift of chastity within marriage, expressed through the free sexual intimacy of husband and wife.

We were created out of God's love for us, and we inherited the desire to love from God himself. We debunk Screwtape every time we perform acts of charitable sacrifice in service to our spouses, family members, or friends without any expectation of receiving anything in return. Acts of service are very important within the Sacrament of Holy Matrimony. The authentic love of spouses is sacrificial in nature and gives without expecting to be served in return.

Within the structure of the marital covenant, the virtue of love is first properly directed toward God the Father, then to the love of the spouses, and last, to the love of children. This threefold gift of the self lays a strong foundation for holy matrimony between man and woman. The union between man and woman in marriage is indissoluble — it cannot be broken.

APPLICATION OF THE *CATECHISM*

The gift of conjugal love between a man and woman in marriage is holy and righteous and demands mutual fidelity. Man need not be a lustful animal if he understands the truth, beauty, and goodness of sex between married spouses: "By its very nature conjugal love requires the inviolable fidelity of the spouses. This is the consequence of the gift of themselves which they make to each other. Love seeks to be definitive; it cannot be an arrangement 'until further notice'" (CCC 1646). These are words that would make Screwtape squirm with spiritual indigestion.

Marriage is an intimate union between two persons who mutually give of themselves in love. The gift of sexual intimacy expresses their love for one another and the love of children. "*Sexuality* affects all aspects of the human person in the unity of his body and soul. It especially concerns affectivity, the capacity to love and to procreate, and in a more general way the aptitude for forming bonds of communion with others" (2332).

DISCUSSION QUESTIONS

- Why does the Church teach that sex is a gift?
- How does a person walk away from lustful sexual desires?
- Why is the gift of sex reserved for the Sacrament of Holy Matrimony?

• • • • •

MEDITATION

(St. John of the Cross, Romance 4)

Then to a deathless music sounding,
Bride to Bridegroom will be pressed,
Because He is the crown and headpiece
Of the Bride that He possessed.
To her beauty all the members
Of the just He will enlace
To form the body of the Bride
When taken into His embrace.

Chapter 19
Understanding Divine Love

His divine power has granted to us all things that pertain to life and godliness, through the knowledge of him who called us to his own glory and excellence, by which he has granted to us his precious and very great promises, that through these you may escape from the corruption that is in the world because of passion, and become partakers of the divine nature.

— *2 Peter 1:3–4*

> *I slipped by mere carelessness into saying that the Enemy really loves humans. That, of course, is an impossibility. He is one being, they are distinct from Him. Their good cannot be His. All His talk about Love must be a disguise for something else — He must have some* real *motive for creating them and taking so much trouble about them. … Leave them to discuss whether "Love," or patriotism, or celibacy, or candles on altars, or teetotalism, or education are good or bad. Can't you see there's no answer?*
>
> The Screwtape Letters, 19

Screwtape would have us believe that God cannot love creatures that are not like Him. His statement deliberately avoids the fact that God is love. For Screwtape, God is God, so why would he bother to love a being not of his own stature? Screwtape views God's infinite love toward man as nothing more than a disguise.

An important point in this letter is the urgency Screwtape exhibits to force the patient to decide whether his own love can be considered good or evil. He wants to cloud the patient's intellect and will by encouraging him to view love in a cynical or gullible way. If the patient does indeed begin to view love as something separate from God, then he will believe that love is nothing more than a human act, not a virtue that we receive from God, and that leads toward God.

DEBUNKING SCREWTAPE

"For God so loved the world that he gave his only-begotten Son, that whoever believes in him should not perish but have eternal life" (Jn 3:16). The words of Saint John's Gospel perfectly summarize God's love for mankind revealed through the death of his Son Jesus Christ. God offered us his Son, and Jesus Christ freely offered himself by dying to save humanity from sin and death. This is the distinctive characteristic of God's love for us: There is no greater love than to lay down your life for someone.

Screwtape's inability to understand God's infinite love is his greatest downfall, just like his father, the Devil. Jesus' sacrificial death on the cross reveals God's love for us, and his desire that we know him more intimately through his Son Jesus Christ.

APPLICATION OF THE *CATECHISM*

God's love is everlasting, and "compared to a father's love for his son. … Stronger than a mother's for her children. … More than a bridegroom [for] his beloved" (CCC 219). He expresses his love through his Son Jesus Christ, whom he gave up for our sins, showing his love for us "while we were yet sinners" (604).

Regardless of our own moral state in life, He will love us to the very end (see Jn 13:1). Hence, no matter how many times the Devil may attempt to convince us that we are incapable of understanding God's love, we need only turn to Jesus Christ, who is love eternal, in order to prove him wrong.

One way we can show God's love to our neighbors is through our participation in the spiritual works of mercy: "Instructing, advising, consoling, comforting are spiritual works of mercy, as are forgiving and bearing wrongs patiently" (CCC 2447). These acts of faith provide us with an opportunity to reflect God's divine love to others through our own acts of love.

DISCUSSION QUESTIONS

- How does sin prevent me from accepting God's love?
- How can the spiritual works of mercy strengthen my relationship with God?
- What does it mean that there is no greater love than to lay down your life for your friends?

• • • • •

MEDITATION

Bl. Solanus Casey wrote five "means for acquiring the love of God" in a personal notebook. These five steps can provide a helpful starting point for all of us:

1. Detachment of oneself from earthly affections — singleness of purpose
2. Meditation on the Passion of Jesus Christ
3. Uniformity with the Divine Will
4. Mental prayer — meditation and contemplation
5. Prayer — "Ask and it shall be given to you"

Chapter 20
Lust

You have heard that it was said, "You shall not commit adultery."

— *Matthew 5:27*

> *The aim is to guide each sex away from those members of the other with whom spiritually helpful, happy, and fertile marriages are most likely. ... There is one type for which his desire is ... readily mixed with charity, readily obedient to marriage ... there is another type which he desires brutally, and desires to desire brutally, a type best used to draw him away from marriage altogether but which, even within marriage, he would tend to treat as a slave, an idol, or an accomplice.*
>
> The Screwtape Letters, 20

In this chapter, Screwtape's intention is to guide the patient into falling in love with the wrong woman. The premise here is that if the patient is going to fall in love with a woman, Screwtape would prefer the wrong type of woman based on purely physical, sexual desires. This would make the marriage untenable because of the man's unrealistic physical desires. He does not want the patient to fall in love with a woman who will provide him with a spiritually holy and happy marriage. Screwtape would prefer a lifelong marriage of misery using man's sexual desires as his own downfall.

DEBUNKING SCREWTAPE

All of us possess inherent dignity as children of God. The Devil knows this and detests the fact that we are created in God's image and likeness. At every turn, the Devil will try to tempt us to abuse our identity as God's children. One way he does this is in how we engage in relationships with members of the opposite sex — either morally or lustfully. We can thwart the Devil's plan by acknowledging and respecting the masculine dignity of every man and feminine dignity of every woman we encounter.

It is important that we discern our relationships through the lens of Jesus Christ and not the lens of our own human desires, asking only, "What can I get out of this relationship?" Our desire for human companionship should be directed toward the virtues of charity, temperance, faith, and sacrifice. A meaningful relationship is built on trust, honor, and respect for the dignity of the person.

Though we are wounded by original sin and weakened by concupiscence, we do not have to be slaves to sin. Our desire for human relationships and intimate companionship does not need to fall strictly under the definition of satisfying one's sexual desires. The journey of acquaintance, courting, friendship, engagement, and ultimately marriage can and should be built on a mutual understanding of sacrificial love of spouses toward one another.

APPLICATION OF THE *CATECHISM*

The *Catechism* tells us, "From a valid marriage arises *a bond* between the spouses which by its very nature is perpetual and exclusive; furthermore, in a Christian marriage the spouses are strengthened and, as it were, consecrated for the duties and the dignity of their state *by a special sacrament*" (1638).

Further:

> By reason of their state in life and of their order, [Christian spouses] have their own special gifts in the People of God.' This grace proper to the sacrament of Matrimony is intended to perfect the couple's love and to strengthen their indissoluble unity. By this grace they 'help one another to attain holiness in their married life and in welcoming and educating their children. (1641)

Finally, the *Catechism* teaches:

> The love of the spouses requires, of its very nature, the unity and indissolubility of the spouses' community of persons, which embraces their entire life: "so they are no longer two, but one flesh." They "are called to grow continually in their communion through day-to-day fidelity to their marriage promise of total mutual self-giving." This human communion is confirmed, purified, and completed by communion in Jesus Christ, given through the sacrament of Matrimony. It is deepened by lives of the common faith and by the Eucharist received together. (1644)

DISCUSSION QUESTIONS

- Why is it important to prayerfully discern before engaging in any type of human relationship?
- How can the virtue of charity help me respect a person of the opposite sex?

› Why is developing a genuine friendship important in a relationship?

• • • • •

MEDITATION

(St. John Chrysostom)

> I have taken you in my arms, and I love you, and I prefer you to my life itself. For the present life is nothing, and my most ardent dream is to spend it with you in such a way that we may be assured of not being separated in the life reserved for us. … I place your love above all things, and nothing would be more bitter or painful to me than to be of a different mind than you.[‡]

‡ St. John Chrysostom, *Hom. in Eph.* 20, 8, PG 62, 146–147, quoted in CCC 2365.

Chapter 21
A Clouded Intellect

Are you also still without understanding?

— Matthew 15:16

> *Now you will have noticed that nothing throws him into a passion so easily as to find a tract of time which he reckoned on having at his own disposal unexpectedly taken from him. ... You must therefore zealously guard in his mind the curious assumption, "My time is my own." ... The sense of ownership in general is always to be encouraged. ... Much of modern resistance to chastity comes from men's belief that they "own" their bodies.*
>
> The Screwtape Letters, 21

Screwtape wants Wormwood to encourage the patient to hold the belief "My time is my own." If the patient believes he is in control of his own time, then no one else's time will hold the same value. Screwtape intends to help the patient develop a sense of personal entitlement, which will cloud his intellect and judgment, especially when things do not go his way.

Screwtape wants Wormwood to use the patient's natural desire for control and ownership against him. He extends this idea not only to time but also to the patient's body. If he believes that he owns his own body, the thought of sacrificing his health or life for someone else would become anathema. This presumption of personal ownership can foster sins of pride, envy, and sloth, which lead to spiritual confusion.

DEBUNKING SCREWTAPE

Freedom is a precious gift from God that allows us to choose to live in communion with him. This gift allows us to take some ownership of our lives through the exercise of our own free will. Yet we misuse this gift, and this misuse dates back to the Fall of man. When the Devil encouraged Adam and Eve to disobey God's command not to eat the fruit from the tree of knowledge of good and evil, he presented them with a false sense of entitlement or ownership.

Our human actions have consequences, both good and bad, for ourselves and those around us. Every human action is driven by our intellect and will. When we conform our intellect and will to God, then we perform good works as disciples of Jesus Christ. Personal ownership that is ordered toward the moral good and centered on God respects the dignity of the human person. It leads us to use our time and our bodies in unselfish ways. But when we have a sense of entitlement, our intellect and will become clouded. Entitlement distorts our view of human freedom and leads to a lack of respect for other human beings.

APPLICATION OF THE *CATECHISM*

Part of the gift of freedom is accepting ownership of our actions. The *Catechism* reminds us that "freedom is the power, rooted in reason and will, to act or not to act, to do this or that, and so to perform deliberate actions on one's own responsibility" (1731).

We all have a responsibility to take ownership of our actions and thus be responsible for our own actions.

> To human beings God even gives the power of freely sharing in his providence by entrusting them with the responsibility of "subduing" the earth and having dominion over it. God thus enables men to be intelligent and free causes in order to complete the work of creation, to perfect its harmony for their own good and that of their neighbors. Though often unconscious collaborators with God's will, they can also enter deliberately into the divine plan by their actions, their prayers, and their sufferings. They then fully become "God's fellow workers" and co-workers for his kingdom. (307)

DISCUSSION QUESTIONS

- How does having a properly formed intellect and will help us take proper moral ownership of our actions?
- In what ways can we resist the temptation to serve ourselves instead of serving others?
- How does the desire to meet our own needs negatively affect our relationship with God?

• • • • •

MEDITATION

(St. Teresa of Calcutta)

> At the end of life, we will not be judged by how many diplomas we have received, how much money we have made, how many great things we have done. We will be judged by, "I was hungry, and you gave me something to eat, I was naked and you clothed me. I was homeless, and you took me in."

Chapter 22
Witness

He came for testimony, to bear witness to the light.

— John 1:7

> *So! Your man is in love. ... I have looked up this girl's dossier and am horrified at what I find. Not only a Christian but such a Christian. ... [The Enemy] has filled His world full of pleasures. There are things for humans to do all day long without His minding in the least — sleeping, washing, eating, drinking, making love, playing, praying, and working. Everything has to be* twisted *before it's any use to us.*
>
> The Screwtape Letters, 22

Nothing appears to give Screwtape more displeasure than encountering an active, faithful disciple of Jesus Christ. His worst fears have come to pass — the patient's life has been infiltrated by an active Christian woman for whom the patient has developed a deep affection. As a result, he has begun to change his lifestyle to become a committed Christian.

Screwtape is desperate to convince himself that the patient is naturally vile and hedonistic and that the prayer vigils and spiritual and corporal works of mercy he does are merely a façade that masks his true self. He is determined to remove the influence of the girl over the patient and chides Wormwood that he should have seen this coming because of the girl's active faith.

DEBUNKING SCREWTAPE

All of us possess a unique identity from God as his children. We are created in his image (see Gn 1:27) and thus bear a resemblance to him. Through the Incarnation, Jesus helps us to live according to that image. When we actively choose to live a life centered on Jesus Christ, our behavior, mannerisms, and disposition will reflect Christ.

The Devil does not want us to surround ourselves with God-fearing people, as their example only strengthens our resolve to live our lives according to the Gospel of Jesus Christ. In this chapter, Screwtape is upset by the holy witness of the young lady to the patient. We are all called to be holy witnesses to others, and we do this first by turning away from sin and seeking an intimate relationship with Jesus Christ for ourselves.

APPLICATION OF THE *CATECHISM*

We are called to be authentic witnesses of the Gospel. When we live this call faithfully, we become witnesses to the Resurrection, the hope that is found in Jesus Christ. Another aspect of authentic witness is our active participation in the sacramental life of the Church (see CCC 1124).

It is in the best interest of our souls that we surround ourselves with holy witnesses who lovingly lead us to encounter Christ and strengthen our relationship with him: "Christian communion among our fellow pilgrims brings us closer to Christ" (957). Holy relationships help us avoid giving in to the

Devil's propositions. The true Christian is not ashamed to testify to Our Lord in deed and word.

Saint Peter reminds us:

> And we are witnesses to all that he did both in the country of the Jews and in Jerusalem. They put him to death by hanging him on a tree; but God raised him on the third day and made him manifest; not to all the people but to us who were chosen by God as witnesses, who ate and drank with him after he rose from the dead. And he commanded us to preach to the people, and to testify that he is the one ordained by God to be judge of the living and the dead. To him all the prophets bear witness that every one who believes in him receives forgiveness of sins through his name. (Acts 10:39–43)

DISCUSSION QUESTIONS

- How can the virtuous habits of those around me affect my relationship with Christ?
- How can the sinful habits of others affect my relationship with Jesus Christ?

• • • • •

MEDITATION

(Pope St. John Paul II)

> Do not be afraid to be holy! Have the courage and humility to present yourselves to the world determined to be holy, since full, true freedom is born from holiness. This aspiration will help you discover genuine love, untainted by selfish and alienating permissiveness; it will make you grow in humanity through study and work;

it will open you to a possible vocation to the total gift of self in the priesthood or the consecrated life; it will transform you from being "slaves" of power, pleasure, money or a career, to being free young persons, "masters" of your own life, ever ready to serve your needy brothers and sisters in the image of Christ the servant, to bear witness to the Gospel of love.[§]

§ Pope St. John Paul II, Message to Youth Meeting in Santiago de Compostela, August 7, 1999, par. 3.

Chapter 23
The Corrupted Mind and the Historical Jesus

But when the time had fully come, God sent forth his Son, born of woman, born under the law, to redeem those who were under the law, so that we might receive adoption as sons.

— Galatians 4:4–5

> *A good many Christian-political writers think that Christianity began going wrong, and departing from the doctrine of its Founder, at a very early stage. Now this idea must be used by us to encourage once again the conception of a "historical Jesus." ... In the last generation we promoted the construction of such a "historical Jesus" on liberal and humanitarian lines; we are now putting forward a new "historical Jesus" on Marxian, catastrophic, and revolutionary lines. The advantages of these constructions, which we intend to change every thirty years or so, are manifold.*
>
> The Screwtape Letters, 23

Screwtape concedes that the influence of an intact Christian family may prove challenging as Wormwood seeks to keep the patient from adopting his girlfriend's Christian principles. Screwtape instructs Wormwood that the way to corrupt the mind of the Christian is to corrupt his view of Jesus Christ. If Wormwood can convince the patient that Jesus Christ is nothing more than a historical figure amongst the multitude of influential people throughout history, then Jesus Christ will take on a lesser significance in the patient's life.

DEBUNKING SCREWTAPE

Jesus Christ is the Son of God. He was born of a woman named Mary, who was sinless and freely said yes to the will of the Father, and so she became the mother of God the Son. Jesus came to save humanity from sin and death. Sacred Scripture, Sacred Tradition, and secular history reveal that Jesus Christ is more than simply a historical artifact. He is a living reality, the Son of God, the Second Person of the Blessed Trinity, who makes himself present to us now in the one, holy, catholic, and apostolic Church, and especially in the holy Sacrifice of the Mass. The notion that Jesus is merely a historical figure strips us of the source and summit of the Christian life, the holy Eucharist, where we receive the living God. It also makes the rule of faith irrelevant. If Jesus isn't fully divine, then we don't have to live our lives according to his teachings. We can justify our sins and selfishness.

APPLICATION OF THE *CATECHISM*

The *Catechism* emphasizes:

> We believe and confess that Jesus of Nazareth, born a Jew of a daughter of Israel at Bethlehem at the time of King Herod the Great and the emperor Caesar Augustus, a carpenter by trade, who died crucified in Jeru-

> salem under the procurator Pontius Pilate during the reign of the emperor Tiberius, is the eternal Son of God made man. He "came from God," "descended from heaven," and "came in the flesh." (423)

Jesus is our path to God the Father and our final home, heaven. The more actively we engage in our relationship with the real, living Jesus through the sacramental life, the less our minds can be corrupted by sin or persuaded to regard the Savior as a mere historical figure.

DISCUSSION QUESTIONS

- Why should I confess that Jesus Christ is my Lord and Savior, and not merely a historical figure?
- How can I develop a relationship with Jesus Christ?
- What does it mean to live a Christ-like life?

• • • • •

MEDITATION

(Matthew 5:17–18)

> Do not think that I have come to abolish the law and the prophets; I have come not to abolish them but to fulfil them. For truly, I say to you, till heaven and earth pass away, not an iota, not a dot, will pass from the law until all is accomplished.

Chapter 24
The Dignity of the Human Person

Blessed are the pure in heart, for they shall see God.

— *Matthew 5:8*

> *The new circle in which he finds himself is one of which he is tempted to be proud for many reasons other than his Christianity. ... While the Enemy, by means of sexual love and of some very agreeable people far advanced in His service, is drawing the young barbarian up to levels he could never otherwise have reached, you must make him feel that he is finding his* own *level — that these people are "his sort" and that, coming among them, he has come home. ... You must teach him to mistake this contrast between the circle that delights and the circle that bores him for the contrast between Christians and unbelievers.*
>
> The Screwtape Letters, 24

There are several layers to this chapter that reveal Screwtape's attempt to lead the patient away from Christianity. First, he tells Wormwood to encourage the patient to ignore any feelings of unworthiness around his girlfriend and her family, but to view them as "his sort" of people. Second, he wants the patient to reach false conclusions about the behaviors of the "circle that delights" versus the "circle that bores," so that his Christian identity becomes bound up with the sin of pride.

DEBUNKING SCREWTAPE

Screwtape's attempt to confuse the patient does not take into account the spiritual resiliency of human beings. If we want to avoid the Devil's trap of spiritual confusion, then the Beatitudes are an integral part of strengthening and clarifying our identity as children of God. Every single human being created by God has a desire for happiness (see CCC 1718). True happiness has its origin in God the Father. God places happiness in our hearts as a gift, and we have a responsibility to cultivate it not only within ourselves but within those around us.

Screwtape wants the patient to feel unworthy of his girlfriend while at the same time feeling pride that he now belongs to the Christian "set." The goal is to turn his Christianity into nothing other than a social reality, focused on belonging to the right crowd. The true goal of the Christian life is not to belong to a particular social sphere, but to develop our relationship with Jesus Christ and grow in genuine holiness by following his teachings, especially the Beatitudes.

APPLICATION OF THE *CATECHISM*

The Beatitudes promise us that the pure in heart shall be granted the vision of God (see 1716). We should view the world through a Christian lens and actively serve others as disciples of Jesus Christ. God reveals himself through the Son so we might know how much God truly loves us.

The *Catechism* teaches, "God put us in the world to know, to love, and to serve him, and so to come to paradise. Beatitude makes us 'partakers of the divine nature' and of eternal life. With beatitude, man enters into the glory of Christ and into the joy of the Trinitarian life" (1721).

A sound way of thwarting the Devil is by praying and actively living out the Beatitudes that we encounter in chapter five of Saint Matthew's Gospel. As we grow in the virtues of the Beatitudes, our vision of God will also grow clearer and illuminate the Devil's lies. Through this illumination of faith, we will be able to see the distinction between good and evil and mature in our relationship with Christ.

Every morning provides us an opportunity to embrace anew our relationship with Jesus Christ and anticipate the coming of the kingdom of God. The gift of joy is a grace that God wants to bestow upon us when we serve him. It affirms our own profession of faith in God the Father and opens the door for spiritual renewal. Only in God will our souls be at rest.

DISCUSSION QUESTIONS

- Why are the Beatitudes important in developing a relationship with Jesus Christ?
- How do the Beatitudes help me serve my brothers and sisters in need?
- How do the Beatitudes help me understand the Ten Commandments?

• • • • •

MEDITATION

(St. John Henry Newman)

> Oh that there were such an heart in us, to put aside this visible world, to desire to look at it as a mere screen between us and God, and to think of Him who has entered in beyond the veil, and who is watching us, trying us, yes, and blessing, and influencing, and encouraging us towards good, day by day! Yet, alas, how do we suffer the mere varying circumstances of every day to sway us! How difficult it is to remain firm and in one mind under the seductions or terrors of the world! We feel variously according to the place, time, and people we are with. We are serious on Sunday, and we sin deliberately on Monday. We rise in the morning with remorse at our offenses and resolutions of amendment, yet before night we have transgressed again. The mere change of society puts us into a new frame of mind; nor do we sufficiently understand this great weakness of ours, or seek for strength where alone it can be found, in the Unchangeable God. What will be our thoughts in that day, when at length this outward world drops away altogether, and we find ourselves where we ever have been, in His presence, with Christ standing at His right hand![¶]

¶ St. John Henry Newman, *Spiritual Writings*, ed. John T. Ford (Maryknoll, NY: Orbis Books, 2012), 95.

Chapter 25
Putting on a False Face

Beware of false prophets, who come to you in sheep's clothing but inwardly are ravenous wolves.

— *Matthew 7:15*

> *What we want, if men become Christians at all, is to keep them in the state of mind I call "Christianity And." You know — Christianity and the Crisis, Christianity and the New Psychology, Christianity and the New Order, Christianity and Faith Healing. ... If they must be Christians let them at least be Christians with a difference. Substitute for the faith itself some Fashion with a Christian coloring. Work on their horror of the Same Old Thing.*
>
> The Screwtape Letters, 25

Screwtape is content that the patient will practice Christianity, but with a caveat. He tells Wormwood that the best way to keep the patient from growing in his faith is to include a distraction that parallels the patient's desire to practice Christianity. The aim is to help the patient view his Christianity through a relative lens — to keep the patient distracted as much as possible with other things that he may equate to Christianity, but which are really superfluous add-ons.

Screwtape's intent is to relativize Christianity in the patient's mind to the point where the patient sees no difference between Christianity and the added distraction. Then the patient will grow bored practicing the same faith repeatedly and begin to look for new distractions.

DEBUNKING SCREWTAPE

Jesus Christ, the Son of God, is the ultimate distraction from the world. He offers us hope in a unique way because he freely chose to die for our sins. The way to debunk Screwtape is to place our trust in God the Father and be willing to imitate Christ's suffering. The Gospel of John reminds us, "If you continue in my word, you are truly my disciples, and you will know the truth, and the truth will make you free" (8:31–32). Screwtape and Wormwood will attempt to distract the patient with false ideologies, spiritual premises, and alternative ways to worship in order to distance the patient from God. But God provides us with the armor of truth. His love for us serves as an antidote that helps us overcome the tricks of the Devil, who is the father of lies.

APPLICATION OF THE *CATECHISM*

The *Catechism* reminds us that as

> members of the Body whose Head is Christ, Christians contribute to *building up the Church* by the constancy of their convictions and their moral lives. ... By living with the mind of Christ, Christians *hasten the coming of the Reign of God*, "a kingdom of justice, love, and peace." They do not, for all that, abandon their earthly tasks; faithful to their master, they fulfill them with upright-

ness, patience, and love. (2045–2046)

The virtue of faith is integral in opening our hearts to God and embracing a genuine relationship with him. "The grace of faith opens 'the eyes of your hearts'" (158). The gift of truth is rooted in the virtue of charity, which exemplifies God's unending love for us and allows us to see through lies or deceptions. Charity guides us away from being distracted by lies because "charity is the soul of holiness" (826).

DISCUSSION QUESTIONS

› How can the virtue of prudence help me stay focused in my relationship with Christ and avoid having an attitude of indifference toward the Church?

› What temptations are currently distracting me from God? Am I ready to renounce them in the name of Jesus Christ?

• • • • •

MEDITATION

(Ephesians 4:22–25)

> Put off the old man that belongs to your former manner of life and is corrupt through deceitful lusts, and be renewed in the spirit of your minds, and put on the new man, created after the likeness of God in true righteousness and holiness. Therefore, putting away falsehood, let every one speak the truth with his neighbor, for we are members one of another.

Chapter 26
Unselfishness and False Kindness

Bear one another's burdens, and so fulfil the law of Christ.

— Galatians 6:2

> *Yes; courtship is the time for sowing those seeds which will grow up ten years later into domestic hatred. ... The grand problem is that of "Unselfishness." ... A woman means by Unselfishness chiefly taking trouble for others; a man means not giving trouble to others. ... The erotic enchantment produces a mutual complaisance in which each is* really *pleased to give in to the wishes of the other. ... You must make them establish as a Law for their whole married life that degree of mutual self-sacrifice which is at present sprouting naturally out of the enchantment, but which, when enchantment dies away, they will not have charity enough to enable them to perform.*
>
> The Screwtape Letters, 26

Screwtape makes it quite clear to Wormwood that he takes great pleasure in destroying relationships. His ultimate desire is to drive a wedge between man and woman in marriage, wreaking spiritual havoc by encouraging each to perform selfish acts. Screwtape seeks to foment despair, anger, and selfishness between spouses over unresolved issues between them.

DEBUNKING SCREWTAPE

It is important to affirm our identity as children of God: We were created out of love. According to Screwtape, only women view unselfishness as embracing the troubles or challenges of a person in need, while men view unselfishness as not *causing* trouble for others. While this may not be true to reality, it does highlight ways in which men and women are susceptible to selfishness.

The Devil wants to pervert the minds of men and women and encourage them to satisfy their own pleasures at one another's expense. But all of us are ransomed by the love of God through the saving death and resurrection of Jesus Christ. This is something the Devil cannot undo. The graces of the sacramental life allow us to freely choose to behave unselfishly, which strengthens our relationship with Christ and with one another.

APPLICATION OF THE *CATECHISM*

The *Catechism* reminds us:

> Respect for the human person proceeds by way of respect for the principle that "everyone should look upon his neighbor (without any exception) as 'another self,' above all bearing in mind his life and the means necessary for living it with dignity." No legislation could by itself do away with the fears, prejudices, and attitudes of pride and selfishness which obstruct the establishment of truly fraternal societies. Such behavior will cease only

through the charity that finds in every man a "neighbor," a brother. (1931)

DISCUSSION QUESTIONS

- What are some ways that I can make spiritual and physical sacrifices for my neighbor?
- What should I do when tempted by the sin of selfishness to do something that could hurt another person?
- In what ways can I imitate Christ by serving others?

• • • • •

MEDITATION

(Psalm 119:105–112)

Your word is a lamp to my feet
    and a light to my path.
I have sworn an oath and confirmed it,
    to observe your righteous ordinances.
I am sorely afflicted;
    give me life, O LORD, according to your word!
Accept my offerings of praise, O LORD,
    and teach me your ordinances.
I hold my life in my hand continually,
    but I do not forget your law.
The wicked have laid a snare for me,
    but I do not stray from your precepts.
Your testimonies are my heritage for ever;
    yes, they are the joy of my heart.
I incline my heart to perform your statutes
    for ever, to the end.

Chapter 27
False Spirituality

And when you pray, you must not be like the hypocrites; for they love to stand and pray in the synagogues and at the street corners, that they may be seen by men.

— *Matthew 6:5*

Humans can often be lured into direct disobedience to the Enemy who ... has definitely told them to pray for their daily bread and recovery of their sick. ... But since your patient has contracted the terrible habit of obedience, he will probably continue such "crude" prayers whatever you do. But you can worry him with the haunting suspicion that the practice is absurd and can have no objective result. ... If the thing he prays for doesn't happen, then that is one more proof that petitionary prayers don't work; if it does happen, he will, of course, be able to see some of the physical causes which led up to it, and "therefore it would have happened anyway."

The Screwtape Letters, 27

In this chapter, Screwtape encourages Wormwood to foster in the patient a misunderstanding of the purpose of prayer. If the exercise of prayer only leads a person closer to his own desires rather than allowing him to communicate with God and give proper praise to Jesus Christ, then the person develops a very self-centered, materialistic approach in which prayer becomes only a means to obtain what he desires. By contrast, true prayer speaks lovingly with God and acknowledges him as Lord in a sacrificial way.

Screwtape also wants to convince the patient that the prayer of petition is useless. If the petition is not granted, what's the point of asking? And if it is granted, he can be convinced that the causes were natural and inevitable.

DEBUNKING SCREWTAPE

God never stops speaking to us or calling for us. Our challenge is to respond to His desire to be in communion with us. The Devil understands very well that God will never stop loving his children; this also means He will never stop desiring what is good for us.

When we view prayer as simply a means to obtain favors from God, we lose the opportunity to communicate and build a relationship with him. Prayers of intercession, petition, thanksgiving, or adoration serve as opportunities to communicate intimately with Our Lord. God never ceases communicating with us; the question becomes whether we want to listen to him. When we pray to our Father in heaven, our intention should be to grow in our relationship with him so that we may better understand who we are as his children and prepare to be with him forever in heaven.

When Jesus introduced the Lord's Prayer, He revealed a new way to communicate with God the Father (see Mt 6:7–15), expressing our firm reliance on him for everything. The Devil does not want us to speak with God. If he can convince us that prayer is simply a means to obtain favor with God or to get what we want, then prayer loses its purpose. Even the holy Sacrifice of the Mass can be rendered pointless if we see it only as a way to obtain our own desires from God.

Humility is the foundation of true prayer — a virtue the Devil seeks to destroy. When we pray, we should seek to surrender to the will of the Father and not our own will. Prayer is an act of trust by which we actively seek heaven.

APPLICATION OF THE *CATECHISM*

The *Catechism* defines prayer as "the raising of one's mind and heart to God or the requesting of good things from God" (2559). This means that any form of prayer must be directed to the divine will of God. "Christian prayer is a covenant relationship between God and man in Christ" (2564). Prayer comes from the heart; "it is the *heart* that prays" (2562) and enables us to communicate with Jesus Christ through trusting obedience that does not require or demand an immediate return.

DISCUSSION QUESTIONS

- What is a first step that we can take to develop (or deepen) a faithful prayer life with Jesus?
- How can we avoid being distracted when we pray?
- What are some ways that the Devil uses to distract us from praying to Jesus?

• • • • •

MEDITATION

(Ephesians 4:17–24)

> Now this I affirm and testify in the Lord, that you must no longer walk as the Gentiles walk, in the futility of their minds; they are darkened in their understanding,

alienated from the life of God because of the ignorance that is in them, due to their hardness of heart; they have become callous and have given themselves up to licentiousness, greedy to practice every kind of uncleanness. You did not so learn Christ! — assuming that you have heard about him and were taught in him, as the truth is in Jesus. Put off the old man that belongs to your former manner of life and is corrupt through deceitful lusts, and be renewed in the spirit of your minds, and put on the new man, created after the likeness of God in true righteousness and holiness.

Chapter 28
Preparing for Heaven or Earth

For to me to live is Christ, and to die is gain.

— Philippians 1:21

> *At the present moment, as the full impact of the war draws nearer and his worldly hopes take a proportionately lower place in his mind, full of his defense work, full of the girl, forced to attend to his neighbors more than he has ever done before and liking it more than he expected, "taken out of himself" ... and daily increasing in conscious dependence on the Enemy, he will almost certainly be lost to us if he is killed tonight. ... The truth is that the Enemy, having oddly destined these mere animals to life in His own eternal world, has guarded them pretty effectively from the danger of feeling at home anywhere else.*
>
> The Screwtape Letters, 28

Screwtape instructs Wormwood to encourage the patient's desire for an earthly life versus a heavenly one. He wants the patient to embrace the pleasures of the world rather than anticipate what is to come in heaven. The longer the patient lives, the more time Wormwood has to encourage him to neglect, or better yet shun, his relationship with Jesus Christ and develop an attachment to the world's empty pleasures.

DEBUNKING SCREWTAPE

When Adam and Eve embraced the first sin, they also embraced the false notion that a world apart from God can offer eternal happiness and physical rewards. This is precisely what the Devil would have us believe. He wants us to seek the false pleasures of a world without God. But the Devil realizes that God is the author of life, time, and space, and that human beings are designed to desire him: "The desire for God is written in the human heart" (CCC 27). As Screwtape admits, "The Enemy, having oddly destined these mere animals to life in His own eternal world, has guarded them pretty effectively from the danger of feeling at home anywhere else."

Death eventually comes to us all. We do not know the hour or the day. Our lives will end one day, and on that day, we will face a moral reckoning before God. Jesus Christ introduced a clear understanding of death; through his crucifixion, he defeated sin and death to save us from our own sins. Jesus' death marked a renewed opportunity to be with Our Lord in heaven if we so choose.

Our journey as children of God begins at baptism, which Jesus instituted in the river Jordan to reveal the path to heaven. God wants us to be prepared for heaven, and that is meant to be the goal and purpose of our lives on earth, no matter how long we live. Like Saint Paul, we should foster the Christian desire to depart from the earth and be with Christ (see Phil 1:23). No earthly desire can measure up to the joy of being with God in heaven. At the same time, we have the foretaste of heaven expressed in the liturgy and in Eucharistic adoration.

APPLICATION OF THE *CATECHISM*

The *Catechism* reminds us that there is a communion between the Church in heaven and the Church on earth. We on earth are pilgrims, preparing for our eternal home in heaven (see 954). But after the Fall, the created world's identity as a gift from God was obscured by man's lustful desires for the pleasures of this world.

The *Catechism* continues:

> This perfect life with the Most Holy Trinity — this communion of life and love with the Trinity, with the Virgin Mary, the angels and all the blessed — is called "heaven." Heaven is the ultimate end and fulfillment of the deepest human longings, the state of supreme, definitive happiness.
>
> To live in heaven is "to be with Christ." The elect live "in Christ," but they retain, or rather find, their true identity, their own name. (1024–1025)

Heaven is our ultimate end that fulfills our deepest longing: communion with the Blessed Trinity, the Mother of God, and all the angels and saints. Jesus' death and resurrection opened heaven for us, inviting us to shun the false pleasures of the world and instead look toward being with God for all eternity. We should live every day as if it were our last day, hoping to be at rest with God in heaven.

DISCUSSION QUESTIONS

- How can I prepare myself to be with God in heaven?
- How can regular attendance at Mass and Eucharistic adora-

tion strengthen my desire for heaven?

› In what practical ways can I develop trust in God?

• • • • •

MEDITATION

(Saint Cyprian)

> How great will your glory and happiness be, to be allowed to see God, to be honored with sharing the joy of salvation and eternal light with Christ your Lord and God ... to delight in the joy of immortality in the Kingdom of heaven with the righteous and God's friends.**

** Saint Cyprian, *Ep.* 58, 10, 1, quoted in CCC 1028.

Chapter 29
The Character of Hatred

If you keep my commandments, you will abide in my love, just as I have kept my Father's commandments and abide in his love. These things I have spoken to you, that my joy may be in you, and that your joy may be full.

— *John 15:10–11*

> *But hatred is best combined with Fear. Cowardice, alone of all the vices, is purely painful — horrible to anticipate, horrible to feel, horrible to remember; Hatred has its pleasures. It is therefore often the* compensation *by which a frightened man reimburses himself for the miseries of Fear. The more he fears, the more he will hate.*
>
> The Screwtape Letters, 29

Screwtape directs Wormwood to convince the patient to identify himself with the oppressed but not with their oppressors so that he will not show mercy. However, Screwtape wants most of all for the patient to be engulfed by the sin of unholy fear or cowardice, because the more he fears, the more he will hate.

DEBUNKING SCREWTAPE

Engaging in an act of hatred motivated by fear is not a situation most of us would want to encounter. Fear and hatred tend to work in tandem and blur our identity as children of God, created in his image and likeness.

We are naturally ordered to be good; it takes a great deal of effort and determination for the Devil to guide us to live for something other than God. This is where the virtues of fortitude and prudence allow us to overcome the sins of unholy fear and hatred. Prudence allows us to understand the nature of our hatred and fear and how they affect our relationship with God. Fortitude provides us with the moral and spiritual strength to address and overcome unholy fear and hatred by placing our trust in the will of God and seeking Jesus' healing and protection.

Prudence and fortitude allow us to discern the truth about situations in life and prevent us from acting impatiently and foolishly out of fear and hatred. Hatred coupled with fear only facilitates the Devil's attacks on us. Keep in mind that when the Devil tries to convince us to perform acts contrary to God's love, we can invoke the name of Jesus Christ because Christ has already defeated the Devil through his death on the cross.

APPLICATION OF THE *CATECHISM*

The *Catechism* teaches, "*Human virtues* are firm attitudes, stable dispositions, habitual perfections of intellect and will that govern our actions, order our passions, and guide our conduct according to reason and faith" (1804). "*Prudence* is the virtue that disposes practical reason to discern our true good in every circumstance and to choose the right means of achieving it" (1806). Prudence helps us to ask the question, "What are the ramifications of my actions?"

Although the virtue of prudence helps us understand the

ramifications of our actions, the virtue of fortitude "ensures firmness in difficulties and constancy in the pursuit of the good. It strengthens the resolve to resist temptations and to overcome obstacles in the moral life" (1808).

The *Catechism* says further: "It is prudence that immediately guides the judgment of conscience. The prudent man determines and directs his conduct in accordance with this judgment. With the help of this virtue we apply moral principles to particular cases without error and overcome doubts about the good to achieve and the evil to avoid" (1806).

Jesus reminds us that the way to dispel hatred is to recognize that our own Christian beatitude is to enter into joy with Our Lord (see Mt 25:21–23).

DISCUSSION QUESTIONS

- Why should I pray for the virtue of fortitude?
- How does the virtue of prudence help me understand the sins of unholy fear and hatred?
- Why are our souls ordered to do good acts? Why do we often reject this good?

• • • • •

MEDITATION

(1 Peter 4:7–11)

> The end of all things is at hand; therefore keep sane and sober for your prayers. Above all hold unfailing your love for one another, since love covers a multitude of sins. Practice hospitality ungrudgingly to one another. As each has received a gift, employ it for one another, as good stewards of God's varied grace: whoever speaks, as one who utters oracles of God; whoever renders service, as

one who renders it by the strength which God supplies; in order that in everything God may be glorified through Jesus Christ. To him belong glory and dominion for ever and ever. Amen.

Chapter 30
Lord, Help Me Persevere

The L*ORD* *is my strength and my song;*
he has become my salvation.

— Psalm 118:14

> *Probably the scenes he is now witnessing will not provide material for an* intellectual *attack on his faith. ... But there is a sort of attack on the emotions which can still be tried. It turns on making him* feel, *when first he sees human remains plastered on a wall, that this is "what the world is* really *like" and that all his religion has been a fantasy.*
>
> The Screwtape Letters, 30

Screwtape instructs Wormwood in ways to use the patient's fatigue to cause spiritual and mental incoherence. Fatigue is the Devil's friend. As man tires, his faculties become disoriented, and his ability to combat the temptations of the Devil weakens, hence he is unable to persevere.

Screwtape also encourages Wormwood to place doubt in

the patient's mind due to the calamities happening around him. Against the backdrop of a world war, Screwtape hopes to cause the patient to feel that religion is useless and cannot help him persevere through the calamities of daily living.

DEBUNKING SCREWTAPE

Screwtape believes that seeing how bad the world is will cause the patient to give up on religion altogether. However, Screwtape underestimates the spiritual temperament of the patient and the grace God gives him to persevere in faith. The gift of faith allows us to invite Our Lord into our daily living and gives us the strength to persevere and to withstand the temptations of the Devil.

APPLICATION OF THE *CATECHISM*

The *Catechism* tells us, "To live, grow, and persevere in the faith until the end we must nourish it with the word of God; we must beg the Lord to increase our faith; it must be 'working through charity,' abounding in hope, and rooted in the faith of the Church" (162). We also "hope for *the grace of final perseverance and the recompense* of God [our] Father for the good works accomplished with his grace in communion with Jesus" (2016).

As we begin to understand what it means to carry the cross of Christ in our daily battle against sin and the Devil, we are reminded:

> Our battle has to confront what we experience as *failure in prayer*: discouragement during periods of dryness; sadness that, because we have "great possessions," we have not given all to the Lord; disappointment over not being heard according to our own will; wounded pride, stiffened by the indignity that is ours as sinners; our resistance to the idea that prayer is a free and un-

merited gift; and so forth. The conclusion is always the same: what good does it do to pray? To overcome these obstacles, we must battle to gain humility, trust, and perseverance. (2728)

DISCUSSION QUESTIONS

- How can the gift of faith help me avoid the sin of despair?
- Why is it important that we persevere through faith in Jesus Christ?
- Can you name someone who has spiritually persevered through a difficult situation in life? How did they do it?

• • • • •

MEDITATION

(1 Timothy 1:18–19)

> This charge I commit to you, Timothy, my son, in accordance with the prophetic utterances which pointed to you, that inspired by them you may wage the good warfare, holding faith and a good conscience. By rejecting conscience, certain persons have made shipwreck of their faith.

Chapter 31
Deliver Us from Evil

Deliver us from evil.

— *Matthew 6:13*

> *My dear, my very dear Wormwood, my puppet, pigsnie,*
>
> *You have let a soul slip through your fingers. ... How well I know what happened at the instant when they snatched him from you! There was a sudden clearing of his eyes ... as he saw you for the first time, and recognized that part you had had in him and knew that you had it no longer. ... He is caught up into that world where pain and pleasures take on transfinite values and all our arithmetic is dismayed.*
>
> The Screwtape Letters, 31

In his final letter, Screwtape is livid because Wormwood has lost the patient for good. Screwtape seems to believe that they had the patient in their hands but in the end watched him slip away to the Enemy (God) to embrace a life of grace with God in heaven. The patient reveals what awaits us if we seek a relationship with God, which is eternal life with him in heaven.

From Screwtape's perspective the patient is now lost forever because he has been embraced by God in heaven. Screwtape is resigned to admit defeat and move on from his loss. However, in classic Screwtape fashion, he still wants to find out what God is up to.

DEBUNKING SCREWTAPE

Screwtape fails to recognize that Jesus Christ always has the last word. He has already won the victory over the Devil by his death on the cross for the salvation of man, and his resurrection gives us hope of joining him in our eternal home in heaven. Jesus fought the good fight of faith and completed his earthly mission to save us from the evils of sin and death.

The important thing to understand in the last stage of this drama is that God never left his own child. Though temptation may appear to reign throughout our lives, God's love and mercy through his Son Jesus Christ are greater. God wants us to have a relationship with him, while the Devil wants the opposite: to isolate us from God.

The Devil no longer has power over us once we encounter the Risen Lord in heaven. As our life expires on earth, through God's grace and the exercise of our own free will, we are able to experience a peaceful and joyful death.

APPLICATION OF THE *CATECHISM*

The last petition of the Our Father is a prayer for deliverance, specifically asking God to deliver us from the wicked snares and spiritual entrapments of the Devil. It is also a petition for protection. "In this petition, evil is not an abstraction, but refers to a person, Satan, the Evil One, the angel who opposes God. The devil (*dia-bolos*) is the one who 'throws himself across' God's plan and his work of salvation accomplished in Christ" (CCC 2851).

Jesus' death frees us from the corruption of sin and death. His willingness to die for the sins of humanity demonstrates the awesome power of God the Son and his desire to protect us from the wickedness of the Devil. "The Lord who has taken away your sin and pardoned your faults also protects you and keeps you from the wiles of your adversary the devil, so that the enemy, who is accustomed to leading into sin, may not surprise you. One who entrusts himself to God does not dread the devil. 'If God is for us, who is against us?'" (2852).

The *Catechism* offers us one final capstone of Church teaching on death and the deliverance from evil:

> When we ask to be delivered from the Evil One, we pray as well to be freed from all evils, present, past, and future, of which he is the author or instigator. In this final petition, the Church brings before the Father all the distress of the world. Along with deliverance from the evils that overwhelm humanity, she implores the precious gift of peace and the grace of perseverance in expectation of Christ's return. By praying in this way, she anticipates in humility of faith the gathering together of everyone and everything in him who has "the keys of Death and Hades," who "is and who was and who is to come, the Almighty." (2854)

In conclusion, the Book of Revelation reminds us of our final battle:

> And the great dragon was thrown down, that ancient serpent, who is called the Devil and Satan, the deceiver of the whole world — he was thrown down to the earth, and his angels were thrown down with him. And I heard a loud voice in heaven, saying, "Now the salvation and

> the power and the kingdom of our God and the authority of his Christ have come, for the accuser of our brethren has been thrown down, who accuses them day and night before our God. And they have conquered him by the blood of the Lamb and by the word of their testimony, for they loved not their lives even unto death. Rejoice then, O heaven and you that dwell therein! But woe to you, O earth and sea, for the devil has come down to you in great wrath, because he knows that his time is short!" (12:9–12)

DISCUSSION QUESTIONS

- How is heaven going to be our new life with God?
- Why does the Devil lack influence over souls in heaven?
- How did Jesus Christ destroy the works of the Devil?

• • • • •

MEDITATION

(St. Ignatius of Antioch)

> Allow me to follow the example of the Passion of my God. If there is any man who has God within himself, let him understand what I wish, and let him sympathize with me, knowing the things which constrain me.
>
> The Prince of this world wishes to tear me in pieces and twist my mind away from God. Let none of you who are present help him, but be on my side: that is, on God's. Do not speak of Jesus Christ but still desire the world. Let no envy dwell among you.
>
> Perhaps when I arrive I will ask you to save my life. Ignore what I say then, but give me what I am writing to ask you now. In the midst of life I write to you desiring

death. My bodily desires have been crucified, and there is in me no fire of love for material things. Within me there is no fire, but only water living and speaking in me, and saying to me from within, "Come to the Father." I have no pleasure in the food of corruption or in the delights of this life. I desire the bread of God, which is the flesh of Jesus Christ, who was of the seed of David, and for drink I desire his blood, which is incorruptible love.

... Pray for me that I may attain my goal. I am writing to you not according to the flesh, but according to the mind of God. If I am given suffering, it will be proof of your goodwill; if it is denied to me, that will be a proof of your disfavor.[††]

†† St. Ignatius of Antioch, *Letter to the Romans*, 6.

About the Author

Dr. Marlon De La Torre is the senior director for the Department of Evangelization for the Diocese of Columbus. His professional catechetical background spans over twenty-eight years, having served as the executive director for the Department of Evangelization and Missionary Discipleship for the Archdiocese of Detroit, diocesan director for Evangelization and Catechesis, chief lay theologian and canonical censor for the Catholic Diocese of Fort Worth, adjunct professor of catechetics for Holy Trinity Seminary, and senior professor of catechesis for the Diocese of Fort Worth Diaconate program.

He served as executive coordinator of the Pastoral Provision in conjunction with the Congregation for the Doctrine of the Faith (Vatican) and the Diocese of Fort Worth. The Pastoral Provision assists Anglican Clergy who wish to serve as priests in the Catholic Church. He has also served as diocesan chair and host of the National Hispanic Encounter (*Encuentro*) conference, adjunct professor of catechetics for Catholic Distance University, and writer for the Augustine Institute's *Symbolon* RCIA and adult education programs.

He served as a parish director of religious education in the Diocese of Youngstown, Ohio, diocesan director of religious education, Catholic high school principal, and dean of catechetics at Sacred Heart of Jesus Catholic High School in the Diocese of

Memphis, and as superintendent of Catholic schools in the Diocese of Kansas City-St. Joseph.

His published works include *Screwtape Teaches the Faith* (TAN/Saint Benedict Press, 2011), *Man Up: Becoming the New Catholic Renaissance Man* (Bezalel Books, 2014), and the *Symbolon* series (Augustine Institute, 2013). He has been a contributing writer for Catholiclane.com, Catholicexchange.com, the *Sower*, catholicmom.com, Catholic News Service, and Newadvent.org. He blogs professionally at knowingisdoing.org.

Dr. De La Torre attended Franciscan University of Steubenville, earning undergraduate degrees in theology and mental health and human services and a master's degree in theology with a concentration in catechetics. He attended the University of Saint Mary in Leavenworth, Kansas, where he earned a master's degree in educational administration and curriculum and a Ph.D. in catholic doctrine, with concentrations in the *Catechism of the Catholic Church*, catechetics, and Catholic education from the University of Notre Dame in Australia.

His most important ministry is his family! Marlon and his beloved wife, Amy, have been married for over twenty-seven years. They have been blessed with seventeen wonderful children — Miguel (twenty-four), Gabriella (twenty-two), Maria (eighteen), Gianna (nine), and thirteen beautiful souls in heaven.